T0171695

Through the Eyes of the Spirit

Living Life with an Uncompromising Perspective

KWAME OWUSU-BAAFI

WESTBOW®
PRESS
A DIVISION OF THOMAS NELSON
& ZONDERVAN

Scripture taken from the Holy Bible, NEW INTERNATIONAL VERSION®.
Copyright © 1973, 1978, 1984 by Biblica, Inc. All rights reserved worldwide.
Used by permission. NEW INTERNATIONAL VERSION® and NIV® are
registered trademarks of Biblica, Inc. Use of either trademark for the offering
of goods or services requires the prior written consent of Biblica US, Inc.

WestBow Press books may be ordered through booksellers or by contacting:

WestBow Press
A Division of Thomas Nelson & Zondervan
1663 Liberty Drive
Bloomington, IN 47403
www.westbowpress.com
1 (866) 928-1240

Because of the dynamic nature of the Internet, any web addresses or
links contained in this book may have changed since publication and
may no longer be valid. The views expressed in this work are solely those
of the author and do not necessarily reflect the views of the publisher,
and the publisher hereby disclaims any responsibility for them.

Any people depicted in stock imagery provided by Thinkstock are models,
and such images are being used for illustrative purposes only.
Certain stock imagery © Thinkstock.

ISBN: 978-1-4908-3783-3 (sc)
ISBN: 978-1-4908-3782-6 (hc)
ISBN: 978-1-4908-3784-0 (e)

Library of Congress Control Number: 2014909201

Printed in the United States of America.

WestBow Press rev. date: 6/2/2014

CONTENTS

PREFACE

ON CHRISTMAS DAY 2006, some members of the communications ministry of our church, the International Baptist Church of Dakar (IBC), got together on the rooftop of a member's house and decided to redesign our weekly bulletin. As part of the redesign, they asked me, as the pastor, to write a compelling, short message for the front page. I started writing these messages by choosing one key word from that Sunday's sermon. The "Word for the Week" was born with regular posts on the pastor's blog section of our website and subsequently widespread dissemination through e-mail distribution lists to friends, families, and former members in Ghana, the United States, and beyond. Feedback from recipients was encouraging, and many began forwarding them to their friends and networks.

As time went on, more stories materialized for each week, more encouraging feedback came from readers and friends, and ultimately a book—this book, my first—developed. It has taken me years to do it, but here we are.

This edition contains fifty-two messages that cover a wide range of heart-related subjects. It is more than a devotional; I have refrained from dating or arranging the messages according to the Christian calendar. It is a reference book for encouragement on any particular subject of the reader's choice at any particular time. At the end of each message, I have included extra Bible passages for further reading and reflection. At the end of each chapter, I have included a short prayer to send the reader to his or her knees.

My sincere appreciation goes to the members of the communications ministry of IBC who started it all and got me to sit down to write what has now become the book in your hands (and others to come). Without that opportunity, I may not have come this far. I cannot help but express my heart-felt gratitude to Amelia Drummond, the current chair of the ministry, who has continued to edit every message before publication in our weekly bulletin. Special thanks also go to my daughter/editor, Afua, for her insights that sharpened the messages she edited, even though she got too busy to continue with the pace as a daily devotional was added to it two years ago. And thanks go to Ama and Afia for working with me on the title for the book, while Sam got me to organize the messages thematically.

And how can I forget my dear wife, Akosua, who has been my constant companion and prayer warrior in ministry? To her I owe my Christian life and journey. And what an exciting journey it has been so far!

To my numerous readers who have read these messages and forwarded them to friends and family, thank you for your comments over the years and your constant encouragement to publish them for a wider audience. You are the reason I am writing today.

The messages in this book have been a tremendous blessing to me personally, and I hope they will bless you as well. I hope they will help us all grow together with a deeper understanding of God's Word as we look *Through the Eyes of the Spirit.*

INTRODUCTION

A TEENAGER APPLIED TO a school for admission and was required to submit a two-page story as part of his application. His story was so good that the principal of the school wanted to meet him upon registration. The following conversation ensued.

> **Principal:** Who wrote this story? The grammar is so poor that I didn't like it at first.

> **Student:** My mother wrote it, and she doesn't have higher education. She is a fishmonger.

> **Principal:** That explains why the paper smelled so much like fish. But I like it because the story is very good and pleasantly insightful, and that's why I wanted to meet and congratulate you. I also wanted to encourage you to take a class in writing that I personally teach because I think you will be a good writer. But since you—

> (The young man, realizing that it was not what he thought but there was a compliment, interrupted.)

> **Student:** Oh, the fish! You see, sir, I had just finished eating the last of the two fish I had stolen from my mother when I sat down to write the story. I guess I forgot to wash my hands well."

Isn't it interesting how we human beings are quick to take credit for a good work done but are reluctant to take responsibilities for our mistakes? We point fingers at others and shift blame on them, taking cover under their ignorance and disadvantaged positions in life. But as the Word of God says, "Nothing in all creation is hidden from God's sight. Everything is uncovered and laid bare before the eyes of him to whom we must give account" (Heb. 4:13). Our deeds will always be shown for what they really are, if not here on earth then surely when the day brings them "to light" (1 Cor. 3:13). The young man was caught in his schemes to get admission into the school in a way he never imagined.

Stories like this young man and the fish are very effective in conveying the thoughts of a writer and help bring meaning to the hearer or reader. That's why Jesus employed it so effectively in the many parables He told. Likewise, many stories told in the form of illustrations have carried countless sermons very well and have brought meaning to the messages preachers have set out to bring to their congregation.

With this in mind, I have employed many stories in this book to carry God's Word to you in a refreshing way. My heart's desire is that these messages will bless many people like you, as far and as wide as the Lord will carry the book, and that glory and honor will rise to Christ when a soul is saved or a life is transformed. Then the mission I set for myself in Bible school—"to challenge myself and others to a greater obedience of God's Word and reverence for His majesty"—would have been achieved in some measure.

CHAPTER 1

Grace

1

Simply Grace

> For who makes you different from anyone
> else? What do you have that you did not
> receive? And if you did receive it, why do
> you boast as though you did not?
> —1 Corinthians 4:7

CHRIS HAD BECOME a very successful entrepreneur right out of college and had been predicted by many to become the richest man in his country in the near future. On this Saturday morning, the family met over dinner to celebrate the ninetieth birthday of their father. Mac, his older brother, had struggled to find his feet in the job market and took the opportunity to make an appeal to Chris for a job with one of his companies. Mac had some personal challenges and was finding it difficult to hold down a job. Chris had been waiting for this opportunity, so he pounced on Mac and dressed him down very well. Chris boasted about his achievements, stressing his ingenuity, initiative, and hard work—the qualities, he said, that had carried him to success.

The old man shifted uneasily in his seat and with a smile told Chris what none of them knew until then. Chris, the old man said, was the most vulnerable and unintelligent of all his children, so he decided to prop him up very early. While he was in college, he engaged a professor to sell the idea of his business to him. It was the old man's own business idea with a well-developed business plan. The professor was to make sure that Chris bought into the idea and signed up for special entrepreneurship training right after college. Dad had arranged for someone to coach him through the development process, a bank to provide the capital, and a major customer for his products. Even the factory manager, accountant, and marketing director had been handpicked by Dad and suggested by the bank as a condition for the loan. "And so, Chris," Dad concluded, "it has all been a special favor from me, so you do not have to boast about anything. Your brother also deserves your favor."

Many times, we want the world to think that every success in our lives has been of our making, so we brag and belittle others. We forget that, out of His love for us, our heavenly Father has freely given everything to us, including our lives. That's why Paul asked in 1 Corinthians 4:7, "For who makes you different from anyone else? What do you have that you did not receive? And if you did receive it, why do you boast as though you did not?"

Our lives are all because of our gracious God, who has freely saved us through faith in Christ Jesus (Eph. 2:8, 9). He requires that we acknowledge this, so freely give to others in need. However, we have set Him aside and instead worship our achievements. We trample each other to show off our abilities and trumpet our accomplishments. But just as Chris' father had graciously worked all those things out for him, so has God's special favor been poured on our lives.

Therefore, the next time you are tempted to say to yourself, "What a man/woman I am," check yourself and know that it is simply grace—God's grace. "For it is by grace you have been saved, through faith—and this not from yourselves, it is the gift of God—not by works, so that no one can boast" (Eph. 2:8–9). So be humble, as Paul said in Philippians 2:3–4, and graciously consider the interest of others, just as Christ Jesus has blessed you with Himself. Acknowledge Him as God's grace offering to you (Titus 2:11–13), and honor Him with your life in that way.

For Reflection

Mephibosheth bowed down and said, "What is your servant, that you should notice a dead dog like me?"
—2 Samuel 9:8

Prayer

There is nothing I deserve but what Your grace has given me. There is nothing I can work for but what You have blessed me with. This is nothing I can pay for but what You tell me, "You can have it." That's how amazing Your grace is, and I embrace it and will never let it go. Help me, oh Lord, never to boast in anything but Christ Jesus alone. Amen!

CHAPTER 2

Salvation

1

What Does Your Hosanna Mean?

The crowds that went ahead of him and those
that followed shouted, "Hosanna to the Son of
David!" "Blessed is he who comes in the name of
the Lord!" "Hosanna in the highest heaven!"
—Matthew 21:9

JESUS IS THE only person who could embark on a triumphal
procession before the final victory had been declared. A warrior
comes home to such a procession only after victory in battle. For
instance, when David killed Goliath and led Israel in a stunning
victory over the Philistines, he returned home with the army to
a procession of women singing, "Saul has slain his thousands,
and David his tens of thousands" (1 Sam. 18:6–7). Of course,
the sound of it did not go well with everybody, particularly King
Saul, but it was a celebration of a great victory over the Philistines,
the enemies of Israel.

Jesus, the descendent of David, faced a greater task: the rescue
of humankind from sin, which gave Satan control over the hearts
and minds of the human race. The final victory of that war had

to wait until the cross and the affirmation from heaven on the third day, but Jesus rode on a colt into Jerusalem in a triumphal procession, as a king returning from war in victory (Mark 11:1–11). The people shouted, "Hosanna!" which means "save," as they went ahead of Him with palm branches. They received Him as the king who would liberate them from Roman rule and reestablish the glory of David's kingdom. But did they understand what they proclaimed?

Jesus indeed rode into His kingdom, but it was not the physical kingdom, as the people envisaged. He would sit on the throne of their father, David, but not the form they had hoped for. First, the King had to take the place of His subjects and serve their sentence of death on the cross of Calvary. His death on the cross was a sacrifice as much as a war of liberation. It was going to happen in the physical realm, but the real war happened in the spiritual realm. It was spiritual warfare of the highest degree—a war for the salvation of the world—and Israel was the nation through which God chose to do it (Gen. 12:3b).

So as Jesus rode on the colt, as had been prophesied in Zechariah 9:9, the chant of the people became the reality of the chant of the psalmist in Psalm 118:22–27. Yes, the King was going to save the people, but not from the Romans, as they expected; it would be from sin and death into a better kingdom that is everlasting. That reality is what the people missed during Jesus' triumphal entry into Jerusalem, and it is why their chants quickly changed from "Hosanna" to "Crucify Him!" Of course, some commentators have argued that the crowd that shouted hosanna was different from that which shouted for His crucifixion, but the contrast is still there. It cannot be firmly established that none in the first crowd, or those who joined without understanding why they were celebrating, changed their opinion in the process. Human beings are fickle and easy to manipulate in such cases.

The pivotal question this Palm Sunday is what you mean when you shout "Hosanna!" Do you mean, "Jesus, save me from my sins" or praise to the giver of what you want? Is your hosanna a shout of praise to the King eternal for your salvation or a simple and hollow celebration of a religious festival? What do you mean by your chant of "Hosanna"?

For Reflection

The stone the builders rejected
has become the cornerstone;
the LORD has done this,
and it is marvelous in our eyes.
The LORD has done it this very day;
let us rejoice today and be glad.
LORD, save us!
LORD, grant us success!
Blessed is he who comes in the name of the LORD.
From the house of the LORD we bless you.
The LORD is God,
and he has made his light shine on us.
With boughs in hand, join in the festal procession
up to the horns of the altar.
—Psalm 118:22–27

Prayer

Jesus, I hail and praise You—not because of what
I will get from You but because of who You are
and what You have become for me and all who
put their trust in You. Thank You for being my
Savior, Lord, and King; continue to be enlarged
in my heart with each passing day. Amen!

2

The Suffering Servant

They put a purple robe on him, then
twisted together a crown of thorns and
set it on him. And they began to call out
to him, "Hail, king of the Jews!"
—Mark 15:17–18

H AVE YOU THOUGHT through the events leading up to
Jesus' death on the cross? What did He do to deserve the
horrendous physical and emotional abuse He was subjected to in
those final hours of His life on earth? What did He do to deserve
all the suffering they put Him through? Why did He bear them
when He knew He was innocent? Why didn't He complain or
protest? Couldn't He have saved Himself? Why didn't He do just
that as the chief priests, teachers of the law, and elders at the cross
shouted (Matt. 27:41–42)?

Why did He endure the emotional struggle in the garden
of Gethsemane (Matt. 27:34–36)? Why did He go through the
emotional agony of His betrayal by one of His own disciples
(Mark 14:44–45)? How about the pain of being deserted by
His friends when arrested (v. 50) and His denial by His closest
confidant at His trial before the Sanhedrin (vv. 66–72)?

Did He have to subject Himself to the trial before Pilate (Mark
15:1–15)? Who was that dog to sit in judgment of the Savior King?
What authority did he have over the one who created him? So why
did Jesus yield to Pilate's judgment? Did He deserve that humiliation?

How about the soldiers? Why did Jesus allow their mockery in
the Praetorium (Mark 15:16–21)? Can you imagine their pitiable

ignorance as they mockingly dressed Him as a king? Can you feel His pain as the crown of thorns was put on His head and He was hit, time after time, with the staff they put in His hands? Can you hear their demonic shouts of "Hail the king of the Jews" (v. 18)? Can you see Him squirm when they spat in His face (v. 19)? How did He feel when they mockingly fell down in homage to Him? Why did He have to endure all that? Did He deserve any of it?

Can you feel His pain as he carried His cross through the narrow streets of Jerusalem to Calvary? Can you hear the sound of the hammer as it cruelly drilled the metal planks through His hands and feet (Mark 15:24)? To add insult to injury, can you hear the insults of the passersby (v. 29)? Can you see them shamefully shaking their heads as they taunted Him with shouts of "Save yourself" (v. 30)? Do you hear the pathetic chief priests and teachers of the law and their mockery? "He saved others ... but He can't save Himself! Let Him come down now from the cross, that we may see and believe" (vv. 31–32). Oh, really? Couldn't He have done just that? Didn't he have the power to do that? So why didn't Jesus perform one of those miracles? Did He deserve all that?

As you consider those events and try to imagine them, can you see love written all over them? Do you begin to comprehend the meaning of love? Do you sense its power? Do you feel its pulse, its heartbeat, its tenacity, its endurance, and above all, its humility? Can you sense its patience, kindness, selflessness, calmness, protectiveness, trustfulness, hopefulness, and perseverance? Does 1 Corinthians 13:4–7 come alive to you? Have you loved that way before? Have you experienced that love from any human being before?

Can you now understand in a new and fresh way the Word of God as inscribed in John 3:16, one of the most quoted but least understood Bible verses? "For God so loved the world that He gave His One and Only Son that whoever believes in Him shall not perish but have eternal life." And Paul added, "But God demonstrates His love for us in this: While we were still sinners, Christ died for us" (Rom. 5:8).

Have you received this love of God through the suffering servant, His Son, Jesus Christ, for your sake? How do you cherish this extraordinary love by the way you live? Do you love Him as He loved you and endured the cross in your place? Give Him glory today, would you?

For Reflection

> But he was pierced for our transgressions,
> he was crushed for our iniquities;
> the punishment that brought us peace was on him,
> and by his wounds we are healed.
> —Isaiah 53:5

Prayer

How can I forget Your pain and suffering for me when You knew no sin and did not deserve the humiliation You suffered on the cross? Yet I so easily forget and live anyhow, bringing dishonor to Your name, as if You need more. Lord, forgive me. In Your mighty name, I pray. Amen!

CHAPTER 3

Faith

1

Faith Walk: Perseverance Is Key

Therefore, since we are surrounded by such a great
cloud of witnesses, let us throw off everything that
hinders and the sin that so easily entangles. And let
us run with perseverance the race marked out for us.
—Hebrews 12:1

WHEN EVERYTHING AROUND turns negative, how does the
child of God maintain equilibrium? How do you maintain
your vertical view when failure has become your food, when age
is rolling by like a flood, and when you are being crushed under
the weight of family expectations and comparisons with friends?
With the world offering so much sunshine in "paradise," the flesh
desiring attention and satisfaction, and the Enemy ferociously
pushing his agenda as the end time approaches, how does the
child of God keep his faith strong and resilient?

Over the years, countless saints have struggled with their
faith when tough realities of life confronted them. It is the same
in our time. Many of God's children today are struggling as their
faith is challenged by the tidal increase in knowledge through

scientific breakthroughs, technological advancement, diverse philosophical propositions and secular thought, fashion galore, and above all, abject poverty on one hand and increasing wealth and power on the other. However, the true and faithful ones who have stood upon the powerful and immutable Word of God have declared victory in their sufferings and rejoiced in the full assurance of the hope of glory (Col. 1:27). As many, in the past, have anchored their faith upon the truth and infallible Word of God, they have been sustained. And it is the same body of truth committed to us that continues to sustain every struggling believer who takes hold of it.

Walk through the "Hall of Faith" in Hebrews 11, and you will be confronted with evidence of human weaknesses and failures that were divinely transformed into strengths and victories, as they unashamedly embraced God and His eternal purpose and plan for their lives. You will be encouraged by the faith of men like Abel, Noah, Enoch, Abraham, Isaac, Jacob, Joseph, Moses, Gideon, Barak, Samson, Jephthah, David, Samuel, the prophets, and many unnamed women and men as they yielded to God against the world and their circumstances. They all caught the vision of heaven and stood upon the infallible Word of God and His sure promises to conquer their worst fears, declaring victory over their struggles for the glory of God. They overcame because they persevered in their trials. By their examples, we too are encouraged to stand firm for Jesus Christ, our Savior Redeemer, and to overcome for His glory (Heb. 12:1–13). He has given us power and authority over evil forces (Luke 10:19) and power to say no to ungodliness and worldly passions so we can live self-controlled, upright, and godly lives in this present age (Titus 2:11–13) until He returns. John writes that the only victory that overcomes the world is our faith in Jesus Christ (1 John 5:4).

That is why taking a stand for Jesus is not popular in this age and will not win you much applause from family, friends, and society. However, we have no other choice if we are truly His. We have a higher call from God, greater goals to attain in our faith-walk, and a Savior to glorify. We cannot fail Him. We have no excuses for failure, and we cannot blame anyone if we do not persevere and triumph. Rather we should rejoice when our faith is challenged, for trials are designed to develop perseverance in us. And perseverance, when allowed to finish its work, makes us "mature and complete, not lacking anything" (James 1:2–4). That is what sustained the Josephs and Daniels of old, and it will sustain you who desire to glorify Him with your life (Rom. 12:1, 2).

So child of the Most High, stand firm and remain true to your Savior, and be encourage by the hope of glory till final victory dawns on you at His coming. Persevere to the end and encourage some struggling saint along the way for your Father's glory.

For Reflection

But we do not belong to those who
shrink back and are destroyed, but to
those who have faith and are saved.
—Hebrews 10:39

Prayer

I confess my weakness when the storm rages
and the tide rises to overwhelm me. I want to
believe and hold on to You in such situations,

but Lord, my flesh often takes me where I do not want to go. Spirit of God, bear Your fruit of self-control and root it firmly in my heart that I may stand and not fall when the tempests toss and darkness obscures my sight. Let the light of Your countenance beam brightly before me as Your Word floods my soul to refresh and encourage. This I ask in the matchless name of Jesus, amen!

2

Zeal: Do You Have It?

The zeal of the Lord will accomplish this.

—Isaiah 9:7

ZEAL IS THE enthusiasm and passion that drives success and accomplishment! The word itself is beautiful, and it's meaning, refreshing. You either have it or you don't. It reveals the heart of a person for God, an issue, or a project. It defines the energy level that is employed in worship and how you attack an issue or project at hand. Nothing can stand in the way of zeal to discourage or to initiate retreat or abandonment. It is forward looking and bold in its steps. It fires initiative and destroys procrastination in its wake. Its eyes are always set on the goal and the joy of accomplishment. When it goes into overdrive, collateral damage may ensue, so the twin brothers of knowledge and wisdom are its best companions. Its aroma is godly, and its disposition is very positive.

Zeal is as precious as an expensive, sparkling gem. The Lord Himself adorns it in defense of His honor and, as a result, releases compassion to embrace those who are equally zealous for His honor (Num. 25:11). It guarantees the certainty of God's promises, and He declares it in bold affirmation of them (2 Kings 19:31; Isa. 9:7; 37:32). When injustice rules anywhere and He sees no one standing against it, Jehovah adorns His armor for war against it and wraps Himself in zeal as in a cloak (Isa. 59:17). That's the kind of divine passion with which God moves to seek revenge for His abused and bruised children! It is the reason why, when He promised to bring His Son into the world to redeem the oppressed and bring justice to the weary soul, God affirmed by the prophet Isaiah that His zeal will accomplish it (9:7). And indeed, He accomplished it for our deliverance by the virgin birth (Luke 1:34–35; 2:6–7).

But how can such beauty and passion fail to pack any reward in its wings for those who are zealous for God? Jesus Himself showed us how to be zealous for God in His anger against those who had turned the Jerusalem temple into a marketplace (John 2:14–16). His disciples observed and remembered the passion of David in Psalm 69:9, which says, "Zeal for your house will consume me" (John 2:17). And indeed, zeal consumed Jesus on the cross. So for His reward, we read from Philippians 2:9–11,

> Therefore God exalted Him to the highest place and gave Him the name that is above every name, that at the name of Jesus every knee should bow, in heaven, on earth and under the earth, and every tongue confess that Jesus Christ is Lord, to the glory of God the Father.

In the same manner, when a dedicated saint employs and adorns the garb of zeal, it fitly rewards him for God's glory and high honor. It is why the child of God is commanded by Paul, "Never be lacking in zeal" (Rom. 12:11). For when Paul's misplaced zeal (Phil. 3:6) was finally transformed and accompanied by knowledge after His Damascus Road encounter with Christ Jesus, he never looked back but passionately worked and died for the Lord. At the end of his life, Paul could boldly look back and claim victory and look forward to his reward from Christ Jesus (2 Tim. 4:7–8), for whose sake He had lost all things in this world (Phil. 3:8).

So as you examine your Christian life today, can you say you have zeal? Are you zealous for the honor of God? Do you have a passion for Christ and His kingdom? Does it show in your walk with Him? Is it evident in your witness? If so, then you can look forward to the reward Christ Jesus will give you yonder, because of your passion for Him. Never look back. Never grow cold. Never stumble. Continue in your zeal, and let God be glorified in your life!

For Reflection

But whatever were gains to me I now consider
loss for the sake of Christ. What is more,
I consider everything a loss because of the
surpassing worth of knowing Christ Jesus my
Lord, for whose sake I have lost all things.
—Philippians 3:7-8

Prayer

Lord, I must confess that I have not been as
zealous as I should be when it comes to the
things of You. I am weak, Lord. I ask for Your
grace to strengthen me so that I will not allow
the things of this world to continue gaining
strength and further weakening me.

3

Of Promises and Conditions

Then Boaz said, "On the day you buy the land
from Naomi, you also acquire Ruth the Moabite,
the dead man's widow, in order to maintain the
name of the dead with his property." At this,
the guardian-redeemer said, "Then I cannot
redeem it because I might endanger my own
estate. You redeem it yourself. I cannot do it."
—Ruth 4:5–6

K OFI WAS LIVID. If you have ever been disappointed to find
out, in the most critical hour, that the conditions of your bill
of purchase protected the vendor from responsibility for almost
every cause of damage, you could sympathize with Kofi. He had
bought this pricey suit for his kid brother's wedding and had taken
it to the local cleaner for a minor alteration. And now the dry
cleaner had ruined it. He demanded a refund, and the company
accepted to pay for it. A day before the payment, a lady called to
inform him that they couldn't honor the payment. The damage
should have been reported within a certain period of time, but
unfortunately, it had lapsed. Kofi went running to the shop with
his receipt that clearly stated that the company was responsible for
all damages to clothes left in their care without reservation. He
knew he had a strong case, but when the woman at the counter
showed him the fine print behind the receipt, he was shattered.
How could they "hide" such important information on the back of
the receipt, and in such fine print that anyone could hardly read?

It reminds me of the story of Boaz and the unnamed
kinsman redeemer at the city gate of Bethlehem (Ruth 4:1–10).

When Boaz informed this relative that Naomi was selling a piece of land belonging to their deceased brother, Elimelech, he readily accepted to buy it (4b). Having declared his intention to buy, Boaz explained the condition of sale to him: he was obligated to redeem the land with Naomi and Ruth, the two widows of Elimelech, and his son, Mahlon, "in order to maintain the name of the dead with his property" (5). I have tried to imagine the face of this man with some amusement every time I read this passage. The man was quick to put in his bid for the land, but when he learned that it came with a responsibility, a side package of two widows—one old and one young foreigner—he quickly declined, citing the possibility of "endangering [his] own estate" (6). Isn't that hilarious? But isn't that how we deal with God?

We are quick to say, "Amen" and "I claim it," to all of God's promises. But how quickly we back off when we read the conditions attached to them. We relish the blessings, but we shy away from the righteous requirements that come with them. Even though we do not verbalize it, deep down in our hearts, we cite, as our excuse, a possible infringement on our freedoms and enjoyments. What we forget is that there is no resurrection without the cross. There is no promotion without quality work, and that comes with great sacrifices.

Praise the Lord; He does not hide His conditions in fine print as the business world does. They always come right before or after the promise, and in that same font size that cannot be missed.

So every time you claim a promise of God, take the time to check for the condition(s) that comes with it, for it is only in its fulfillment that the blessings will flow unto you and your family in accordance with His sovereign will.

For Reflection

If you do what is right, will you not be
accepted? But if you do not do what is right,
sin is crouching at your door; it desires to
have you, but you must rule over it.
—Genesis 4:7

Now if you obey me fully and keep my
covenant, then out of all nations you will be
my treasured possession. Although the whole
earth is mine, you will be for me a kingdom
of priests and a holy nation. These are the
words you are to speak to the Israelites.
— Exodus 19:5-6

Prayer

Lord, help me to always obey Your Word in full and
to accept the responsibilities that come with Your
blessings. Thank You in the name of Jesus. Amen!

CHAPTER 4

Doctrine

1

Guard the Truth!

Guard the good deposit that was
entrusted to you—guard it with the help
of the Holy Spirit who lives in us.
— 2 Timothy 1:14

TRUTH, THE EMBODIMENT of everything that is the essence of Christ Jesus, has become the number one item on the endangered list of morality. It has been denied, challenged, covered, dressed in different garbs, and vehemently condemned in our time, but hardly is anybody standing up for it. We live in a world where telling the truth may offend somebody and make you the perfect candidate for vilification. Ours is a world of live and let live; don't rock the boat, and you will be fine. So everybody is looking after their own interest (Phil. 2:4). Consequently, everyone is turning a blind eye to the evils of our day (2 Tim. 4:4) as communities and nations are pillaged and dragged into moral decadence and bankruptcy. Sadly, no one is winning, yet we congratulate ourselves as the most civilized people of all time.

At such a time, one would expect that God's children would stand out as custodians of truth. But have you noticed that we have become the worst offenders when truth is at stake? How many of us haven't looked the other way when somebody is living a sinful life? How many of us haven't shut our mouths when the offender is sitting right under our noses? How many haven't protected our jobs, "reputation," or interests by "going along," even when our conscience is strongly protesting? How unfortunate it is, for the one who saved us is the truth (John 14:6) who commands us to let truth undergird everything in our lives (Eph. 6:14).

Cecilia was a beautiful, young Christian woman of excellent witness among her peers. Her best friend, Angela, introduced her to Mark and they got married. Her boss trusted her at work, so he established her on a managerial path with the company. One day, Angela stole a precious item from the company they both worked for and Cecilia asked her to return it. Angela refused. When asked about it personally, Cecilia struggled with her answer, yet for her friend's sake, she denied knowledge of it.

Two months later, Angela got convicted in her spirit during her morning devotion so she confessed to her boss. Her boss asked her just one question: "Did Cecilia know about this?" Angela, unwilling to sin a second time, told the truth. Unknown to Cecilia, she had lost the confidence of her boss, and a brighter future with her company as manager.

Truth is difficult to tell sometimes, especially when it comes close to someone we love. Yet the Lord commands us to tell it at all times (Eph. 4:15). That is what sets us free (John 8:32) and establishes our witness (Prov. 12:17). Without truth, darkness reigns, for truth is Christ and Christ is the light of the world (John 8:12). Trust is absent where truth is sacrificed on the altar of expediency, and life becomes unpredictably dangerous.

That is why Paul counseled his protégé, Timothy, to guard the good deposit, the body of truth that was entrusted to him, with the help of the Holy Spirit (2 Tim. 1:14). When, moment by moment, we yield to the Spirit of truth (John 14:17), we can live by the truth. It is only through diligence in this matter that the child of God can become a holy instrument of change in our churches, communities, and nations.

Remember "You are the light of the world ... [So] let your light shine before men, that they may see your good deeds and praise your Father in heaven" (Matt. 5:14–16).

For Reflection

Instead, speaking the truth in love, we will
grow to become in every respect the mature
body of him who is the head, that is, Christ.
—Ephesians 4:15

Prayer

You, who are the truth, help me to love to tell the
truth all the time so that I will be a true reflection
of Your heart wherever I may be. Thank You,
Father, for giving us Your Son so that we may
know the truth and be set free, and so that we
may set others free by speaking the truth in love.

2

Human Preferences and God's Choices

> Isaac said, "Prepare me the kind of tasty food
> I like and bring it to me to eat, so that I may
> give you my blessing before I die ... Rebekah
> said to her son Jacob ... 'I can prepare some
> tasty food for your father, just the way he likes
> it. Then take it to your father to eat, so that he
> may give you his blessing before he dies.'"
> —Genesis 27:2–10

WHY DID ISAAC ask Esau to go hunting and prepare his favorite meal for him before he blessed him? Was it a play on what took place between Esau and Jacob when the older brother exchanged his birthright for a bowl of red stew? Was Isaac asking Esau to buy back his rightful paternal blessing with the "food" for which he exchanged his birthright with Jacob? Or did Isaac want his heart to be content with the "kind of tasty food [he liked]" (Gen. 27:4) before blessing Esau? Whatever his reason, it is quite clear that Isaac had a special liking for Esau. For despite God's Word (Gen. 25:23) and Esau's aloofness about his birthright (29–33), Isaac did everything to bless him over Jacob.

On the other side of the family, we meet Rebekah, the mother of the twin brothers. She was so worried about the jostling between the two boys in her womb that she inquired of the Lord about it. God told her that she was carrying two nations that would be separated. One would be stronger than the other, and "the older would serve the younger" (25:23). Probably based on this information, Rebekah watched over Jacob's life with keen eyes to ensure that God's Word would be fulfilled in him. To that extent, Rebekah was prepared to be cursed by helping Jacob get the paternal blessing, rather than Esau (27:13).

See how far we can go to "help" God bring His promises to pass? Was it not the same with Sarah and Abraham, and is it not the same with us today? Don't we take certain crocked actions and compromises to ensure the fulfillment of God's promises in our lives?

But what was God's will in all of these intrigues? Did He also play favoritism in this matter (Gen. 25:23)? That question stretches the query to address God's acceptance of Abel over Cain, Isaac over Ishmael, Joseph over his older brothers, as well as David over his. The key to understanding these choices lies in His election plan (Rom. 8:29–30). Paul reveals this clearly in 9:12–16. "Yet, before the twins were born or had done anything good or bad—in order that God's purpose in election might stand: not by works but by him who calls—she was told, 'The older will serve the younger.' Just as it is written: 'Jacob I loved, but Esau I hated.'"

In other words, God's eternal plan of grace is not determined upon natural right as Esau, being the firstborn son, could claim. On the contrary, God freely gives according to His sovereign choice. His blessing is purely by grace. That's why the new birth does not depend on any "natural descent, a human decision, or a husband's will, but … of God" (John 1:13). It is also "not by works, so that no one can boast" (Eph. 2:9). So Isaac and Rebekah may have had their preferences and choices, but God had the last word. In all of their jostling and scheming, God was working His eternal plan and purpose for our good in Christ (Rom. 8:28).

In the same way, we too can have our preferences in the family or in any other setting; ultimately, God's Word will prevail. His choices will always triumph over human choices; His plan and purpose in every situation will always prevail. It has nothing to do with human wisdom or strength (1 Cor. 1:26–31).

So don't worry about the human intrigues and schemes around you. Don't worry about your parents' preferences and their hurtful words spoken against you as a child. Don't let your boss' partiality against you cause you to be angry and bitter (Heb. 12:15–17). Nor should you allow sibling rivalry to mess up your mind. It may be painful and wicked, but God's plan for your life will ultimately prevail (Jer. 29:11).

For Reflection

For those God foreknew he also predestined to be
conformed to the image of his Son, that he might be
the firstborn among many brothers and sisters. And
those he predestined, he also called; those he called,
he also justified; those he justified, he also glorified.
—Romans 8:29–30

Prayer

Help me, oh, Lord, to accept Your sovereign
plan and rule over my life. Then I will not be
overcome by the intrigues of men. I pray that
in every situation, I will see Your providential
hand at work in my life. May Your grace carry
me through each step of the way through all
of life's treacherous path, in Jesus' name.

3

You Are Human; He Is God!

So Jezebel sent a messenger to Elijah to say, "May
the gods deal with me, be it ever so severely, if
by this time tomorrow I do not make your life
like that of one of them." Elijah was afraid and
ran for his life ... He came to a broom bush,
sat down under it and prayed that he might
die. "I have had enough, LORD," he said. "Take
my life; I am no better than my ancestors."
—1 Kings 19:2–4

HAVE YOU EVER wondered why the prophet Elijah ran for
his life when Queen Jezebel threatened on oath by her
disgraced gods to kill him, as he had slaughtered the prophets of
Baal and Asherah? Or let me bring it closer home to you. Why do
you fear and shudder when you are confronted by a situation even
after God has worked a mighty deliverance or miracle in your life?
Why do you get anxious when God's power to deliver and provide
is all over your life? The fact of the matter is that you, Elijah, and
I are one and the same kind: very human and frail. We constantly
need something to remind us of the truth that we are human and
only He is God. This way, we would not be puffed up and think
for one second that by our own power, we have done something
that God has enabled.

Elijah had prayed and shut the heavens from giving "neither
rains nor dew" (1 Kings 17:1) for three and half years (James 5:17)
because of the idolatry that King Ahab, and his wife, Jezebel, had
caused Israel to embrace. He had been fed by ravens (2–6), and
when the brook dried, by a widow in Zarephath (7–16). He had

raised the widow's dead son (17–24), and Jehovah had answered Elijah's prayer and consumed his sacrifice by fire from heaven in the contest on Mount Carmel (38). The people had responded in affirmation that the Lord is God (39), and Elijah had ordered the slaughter of eight hundred and fifty prophets of Baal and Asherah (40). But when Jezebel threatened to kill Elijah, swearing by the same gods who had proved to be no gods on Mount Carmel (19:1, 2), the prophet became afraid and ran for his life (3).

Can you imagine that? Such a "powerful man of God" running away from the threat of a woman whose gods could not show up in a "who is who?" contest before the very people she had intimidated by those gods. Where was Elijah's power? Where was his boldness? The reality is Elijah was as human as we all are (James 5:17a) and all his powerful acts had been done by God and not himself.

I am glad that God shows the human side of his heroes in the Bible. I am glad to learn that Elijah ran for his life; that he was intimidated; that he was as human as I am, susceptible to the same fears and intimidations as other human beings; and that Elijah got so dejected that he prayed for God to take his life. It gladdens my heart to read that Elijah said, "I am no better than my ancestors" (1 Kings 19:4). Reality check, folks! From the mountain into the valley! That's how God humbles His servants.

Remember Paul and his thorn? It was God's instrument to keep him from becoming conceited because of the surpassingly great revelations he had received from God (2 Cor. 12:1–7). "Three times I pleaded with the Lord to take it away from me. But He said to me, "My grace is sufficient for you, for my power is made perfect in weakness" (8, 9). It is grace, my friend! Just by the grace of God.

So before you raise your shoulders and your nose with an attitude like a plane that has just taken off, remember you are human; He is God. And if you are down and fearful because of some threatening situation, remember you are not the first—and certainly not the last—to be there. It shows that you are human. But if you do not give up but are able to lift your eyes and fix them on Jesus, His grace will pick you up, just to remind you that He is God and that all glory belongs to Him.

For Reflection

> Then Job replied to the LORD:
> "I know that you can do all things;
> no purpose of yours can be thwarted.
> You asked, 'Who is this that obscures
> my plans without knowledge?'
> Surely I spoke of things I did not understand,
> things too wonderful for me to know.
> "You said, 'Listen now, and I will speak;
> I will question you,
> and you shall answer me.'
> My ears had heard of you
> but now my eyes have seen you.
> Therefore I despise myself
> and repent in dust and ashes."
> —Job 42:1–6

> Oh, the depth of the riches of the
> wisdom and knowledge of God!
> How unsearchable his judgments,
> and his paths beyond tracing out!
> Who has known the mind of the Lord?
> Or who has been his counselor?

Who has ever given to God,
that God should repay them?
For from him and through him
and for him are all things.
To him be the glory forever! Amen.
—Romans 11:33–36

Prayer

Lord, I confess that I am human and that You
are God. I am Your creation. All that I am and
that I am able to do comes from You. Forgive
my presumptuous thoughts and haughty claims,
and help me to rely only on You for everything
at all times and in all circumstances. Thank
You, for I have prayed in the name of Your
merciful and compassionate Son, Jesus Christ,
my Lord. To Him be glory forever! Amen.

4

Does Anybody Understand?

And there before me was a throne in heaven
with someone sitting on it. And the One who
sat there had the appearance of jasper and
carnelian ... In the center, around the throne,
were four living creatures ... Day and night they
never stop saying: Holy, Holy, Holy is the Lord
God Almighty, who was and is, and is to come.
—Revelation 4:2–8

As I reflected on the Libyan revolution, I couldn't help
but think about this Scripture. In it, we see the throne of
God in heaven through the eyes of the apostle John. Pondering
its beauty and majesty, I realize that it is the only throne that has
a permanent and enduring occupant: the King of Kings and the
Lord of Lords. Every other throne has a temporary occupant,
according to the will and plan of God.

While I continued in my reflection, I recalled Colonel Gadhafi
sitting on a throne, with a sash and a crown and calling himself
"king of kings." He had enthroned himself as the "king" among
all the kings of Africa, demanding worship in his dream of an
everlasting kingdom. But as I wrote this devotion, images of his
palace being ransacked and trashed by his own people in the final
hours of his forty-two-year reign came flooding into my mind
and I wondered, "Does anybody understand? Can anybody learn
that there is only one who has an eternal throne and everybody
else has a temporary "throne" that has to be abdicated when his
time comes?"

Over the cause of history, upheavals like the Arab Spring, have overthrown kings and presidents and other kinds of leaders who have seen themselves as the ultimate rulers of their nations. They considered themselves "the ones" who alone could, and had, the right to rule, and without them, their nations would collapse or cease to exist. They heaved accolades upon accolades on themselves and assumed titles that proclaimed them gods. Like Hitler, their words struck terror in the hearts of millions, and their commands sent many to their inhuman and brutal end. Somehow, those rulers succeeded in convincing themselves that they were invincible and that nothing could touch them. They lived in a fool's paradise until somebody, or their people, rose up and showed them that they were just as human as everybody else was and that they did not have absolute authority over anyone or anything.

Unfortunately, this demonic trend continues today.

The truth is only one God is sovereign and lives and rules forever. His name is Jehovah, God almighty, whose name is I AM WHO I AM (Ex. 3:14). He rules from heaven. All power and authority come from Him and end in Him (Rom. 11:36), and it is He who "humbles and exalts" (1 Sam. 2:7). He is the "God who judges: He brings one down, and He exalts another" (Ps. 75:7); "the Lord [who] sustains the humble, but casts the wicked to the ground" (Ps. 147:6); the God who "changes times and seasons; He sets up kings and deposes them" (Dan. 2:21). If only men like the late Gadhafi could understand this, they would hold their positions of authority very loosely. The sad commentary is that they don't, and their end has always been brutal.

However, before you condemn the Gadhafis of this world, remember that you could be just like them, for there is a throne you are occupying illegally and are fighting like them to continue to occupy. It is called the heart—the throne from which we all rule over our lives. It belongs to God, your maker, and He wants it back as your Lord and King. He could have chosen to wrestle it from you like all those dictators, but He has graciously given you the opportunity to willingly abdicate it to His Son, Jesus Christ. He stands at the door (of your heart) and knocks, waiting to come and dine with you, if only you will open it to Him (Rev. 3:20).

So will you get off the throne of your life for Christ to occupy and rule over you, or you will fight to continue your illegal occupation like Gadhafi and Idi Amin Dada? Their ends were not pleasant, you know.

For Reflection

In the year that King Uzziah died, I saw the
Lord, high and exalted, seated on a throne;
and the train of his robe filled the temple.
—Isaiah 6:1

God, the blessed and only Ruler, the King
of kings and Lord of lords, who alone is
immortal and who lives in unapproachable
light, whom no one has seen or can see. To
him be honor and might forever. Amen!
—1Timothy 6:14–15

Prayer

Forgive me Lord, for taking Your place on the seat of my heart and making myself the boss of my life and the prophet of my destiny. I cover my face in shame as I behold Your face in Christ Jesus and experience the magnificence of Your glory. I surrender to You now and relinquish the throne of my life for You to occupy and rule in my life. Thank You, in Jesus' name!

CHAPTER 5

Prayer

1

Do You Really Want to See?

"What do you want me to do for
you?" Jesus asked him.
The blind man said, "Rabbi, I want to see."
—Mark 10:51

OFTENTIMES, WE BUY things we do not really have use
for. How many times have you felt the strong urge to buy
something only to use it once and discard it somewhere and not
even remember you have it? Go into some people's closets and you
will be shocked by the number of new and unused dresses you will
find. And yet they have need for more. Why in the world would
anybody spend money to buy things they may never use for years?

There are also many who live in the world of "If only I had this
or that thing, life would be much better for me." They are stuck
in the fairy world of expectations and never get out of it. They
usually do not appreciate what they have, nor have they learned to
use what is within their reach. Yet they expect new things.

I remember a time during my business days when I thought
I would do better if only I had access to credit. A successful

businessman who used our services I approached for a soft loan shocked me out of my dream world. His response went something like this: "May I give you some advice? I come to your place every day and I see a lot of things you don't use much or have never used. Why don't you try to maximize their use first, and if anything is not useful to you now, why don't you sell it and raise the money for your current need?" I must confess I did not take it well at all. I got angry within and thought he was a wicked man who had refused me the little push I needed for a "liftoff." But later, I realized how right he was about the underutilization of what I had and the wisdom in his advice, as well as my slackness and the indolence it inferred. The real question of my life then was this: did I really need what I was asking the loan for, and most importantly, was I going to effectively use it?

I am sure many will dispute my proposition from this discussion that we do not really need most of the things we ask for in prayer. But I sincerely believe that to be the case simply because many of us do not actively and effectively use what God has given us in answer to our prayers.

Consider the spiritual gift God has given you. Aha! I can see that smile on your face. So can I ask a simple question? What are you doing with it, and how effectively are you using it? If God were to evaluate you now in that area, like your boss would do for your request for a raise, do you think you will qualify for another gift? Now, apply that question to every area in your life—marriage, children, job, business, friends, health, and the money in your account you think is too little—and see how your next prayer will sound.

I am sure many of us are angry with God for some supposedly unanswered prayer in the same way I was with my friend who refused me the loan. But of all the many things God has given you, are you appreciative? Do you really need more? Will you use it if God gives you what you are asking for?

Jesus asked blind Bartimaeus, in answer to his plea for mercy, "What do you want me to do for you?" Bartimaeus responded that he needed his sight (Mark 10:51). Jesus gave him his sight, and Bartimaeus "followed Jesus along the road" (v. 52). He used what he received in answer to his request. How about you? Do you really need to see? Will you joyfully use that sight to follow "Jesus along the road"?

For Reflection

So I was afraid and went out and hid your gold
in the ground. See, here is what belongs to you.
—Matthew 25:25

Prayer

Father in heaven, help me to be appreciative of what
You have given me and to use them well for Your
glory. May contentment be my bed and pillow so
that praise will flow out my heart and ascend to
Your lofty dwelling, in the name of Jesus, amen!

CHAPTER 6

Communication

1

Did You Hear Anything?

I pray that the eyes of your heart may be
enlightened in order that you may know the
hope to which he has called you, the riches of his
glorious inheritance in his holy people, and his
incomparably great power for us who believe.
—Ephesians 1:18–19

H EARING IS A very important and vital component of
communication, yet we take it for granted. Even though
many systems and instruments have been invented and created
to facilitate communication, nothing beats the natural ability to
see and hear when communicating with one another, or with
the beauty of nature. Imagine, for a second, walking through a
beautiful tropical rain forest without the sound of those colorful
birds chirping and singing and the sound of the wind whisking
through the giant trees. Or see yourself, for a second, standing
at the observatory of Niagara Falls without the sound of that
huge body of water from Lake Ontario, called the Niagara River,
cascading and tumbling down the cliff of dolostone and shale 167

37

feet into the basin and on into Lake Erie. If these were to happen, the beauty of those scenes would be dulled and the full expression of nature would never be experienced. But the most frustrating and upsetting experience of them all is to talk with the one you love and not be able to hear him or be heard either. For nothing beats the satisfaction of speaking to your spouse, child, or friend, and be assured that you have been heard. Yes, one can read the lips or hear through sign language, but nothing beats the beauty of hearing the voice and expressions of a lover over a candlelight dinner.

That's why Alexander Graham Bell felt so much for deaf people that he devoted himself to help them gain that ability somehow, a passion that led him to his wife, Mabel, who was one of his students. It was his intense passion to give his lover the ability to hear that developed his interest in sound and electricity, and to his invention of the telephone. Yet we who have that ability take it for granted. If "Crazy Bell," as they called him, went to that extent to help his lover to hear him, can you imagine the effort God has put into getting us to hear Him communicate with us?

Our five senses are exactly meant for communicating with God and with one another. That's why when God chose Israel into a special relationship with Him, He desired for them to hear His commands and understand Him, so that they could have good fellowship with Him and with one another and could enjoy His blessings. However, the heartbreak of God was that Israel became a calloused people, so they hardly heard Him with their ears or saw Him with their eyes (Matt. 13:15). Consequently, they did not understand Him with their hearts and turn to Him for healing (15b). What a sad commentary about Israel! Unfortunately, it is the same commentary about the children of the kingdom today. We hear God every day, yet we don't *hear* Him.

You see, many people think that the goal of communication is to speak and be listened to. Nothing could be farther from the truth than that. For communication seeks more than that. It has a greater need embedded at the core of its meaning. It is called understanding; and that is what the speaker seeks from the listener in communication. So, when a speaker thinks that because he has been politely listened to by the audience, and even applauded, he has done a great job, he could be under a strong delusion. All he has done is to demonstrate his lack of understanding of the purpose of communication. Speaking and hearing are the means to an end. The actual end is greater understanding.

In the same way, when God speaks to us, He desires more than having ears to hear. The ability is the means, but understanding with the heart is the focus of God in communicating Himself to us through His word and nature (Ps. 19). That was Paul's prayer for the Ephesians: "that the eyes of [their] heart may be enlightened (Ephesians 1:18, 19). However, because we have allowed sin, the self, and the pressures and enticements of this world to blind, callous, and dull our hearts, we can hardly hear Him, even when we hear the best sermons and memorize all Scripture. We are unable to comprehend His voice in them. No wonder our relationships suffer for lack of proper communication.

My prayer for you this week is that you will rise above the pressures of this world and yourself and practice proper communication with God, taking the time to hear Him with your heart when He speaks, and also your spouse, children, and friends.

For Reflection

Here I am! I stand at the door and knock. If anyone
hears my voice and opens the door, I will come
in and eat with that person, and they with me.
—Revelation 3:20

So, as the Holy Spirit says:
"Today, if you hear his voice,
do not harden your hearts
as you did in the rebellion,
during the time of testing in the wilderness.
—Hebrews 3:7–8

Prayer

Lord, help me to hear You with my heart that I
may know the hope to which You have called me,
the riches of Your glorious inheritance in me, and
the incomparably great power that is at work in
me. Spirit of the living God, open my ears to hear
Jesus knocking on the door of my heart that I
may open it wide to Him for intimate fellowship.
And may You hear me, Lord, when I call. Amen!

CHAPTER 7

Christian Character

1

Would You Step out of the Way?

He must increase, but I must decrease.
—John 3:30

H AVE YOU EVER wanted to do something but had somebody standing in your way and playing interference? It could have been a friend who wouldn't leave or stop talking when you wanted to be alone, an intrusive mother who overextended her visit, or a child who wanted your attention when you were watching the Super Bowl or the finals of the World Cup. Do you remember the night you received an extended call from your boss when the children were asleep and you were making progress with your spouse in bed? Remember when he kept talking as you watched your spouse slip away into a deep slumber? Didn't you feel like screaming, "Get out of my way"? Have you ever considered that you too might be playing interference in the lives of others to the extent that they dread your company? Now, did it ever occur to you that you do the same thing to God all the time? Has it ever crossed your mind that your posture and attitude could be obstructing God's work and plan for your life? Can you hear heaven whisper, "Get out of the way"?

There is the story of a man whose close friend visited at the wrong time of the day. It was suppertime and the meal that day was barely enough for his family to share with his friend. As the conversation lingered and his children kept looking at him, silently pleading, "Daddy, can we eat?" he got exasperated. He excused himself, called his maid aside, and asked her to call his friend's mobile phone and tell him that his house was on fire. Now, that really got his friend out of their way!

Of course, God is not like this brother who couldn't share his meal, but the message is the same. "Get out of God's way!" He wants to do something in your life for His glory, but you are playing interference.

The almighty God wants to talk with you in prayer, but you are too busy making your own plans to listen for His. He desires to share some insights in His Word with you, but you have turned your Bible study time into a ritual. He wants to bless you so that you may be a blessing to others, but you are too busy trying to make it on your own. God wants to reach somebody for salvation through you, but your mind is too far away to notice the critical situation of that person.

When God gave you that college degree and worked you up the career ladder, settling you in that position you now occupy, it was so that you would glorify Him and exalt His name among the people around you. However, you have become so big in those shoes that people can hardly recognize you. You don't have time for Him anymore. He calls you to service in His house, but your calendar is too full to accommodate Him. He calls you to give in support of His work, and you act as if it were your own money. You throw some change at Him with the excuse that the church is overspending. How about your constant complaining and grumbling, the petty jealousies, the nursing of wounds, the bitterness, and the like? How do you think they sound in the ears of God? Remember the Israelites in the wilderness. Their grumbling interfered with God's Canaan agenda for them (1 Cor. 10:10).

Maybe God has to get an angel to call and tell us that our houses are on fire. That, certainly, will get us out of His way. Remember what John the Baptist said. "He must increase, but I must decrease" (John 3:30). The only way to get out of God's way is to let Him have His way in all things. Remember He is the man! You are only a vessel for His service like John was for His coming. When the main character of a play comes, the supporting actors move away into their secondary roles so that the main character will have all the attention of the audience. That's what John was, and that's what we all are.

So can you just step out of the way of Jesus, the mover and shaker of everything that will take place this year, and see Him do wonders in your life? If only you can let Him have all the glory, you will see how much He will bless you.

For Reflection

"For I know the plans I have for you," declares
the LORD, "plans to prosper you and not to harm
you, plans to give you hope and a future."
—Jeremiah 29:11

Prayer

Lord, I acknowledge that You know all things
and that You have a plan for my life. Help me

to empty myself and give You room to fill all of me with Your Holy Spirit. I wholly surrender my life to You, and I pray that even when I feel like things aren't going well, I will stand firm in trusting You. My wisdom is no wisdom at all; help me remember that true wisdom is allowing You to rule over every part of my life.

2

Convictions

I was forty years old when Moses the servant
of the LORD sent me from Kadesh Barnea to
explore the land. And I brought him back
a report according to my convictions.
—Joshua 14:7

I AM ALWAYS fascinated by the story of Caleb. This was a
man who, at the age of eighty-five, asked Joshua to give him
the hill country of Hebron as his inheritance even though the
opposition was formidable (Josh. 14:6–15). Caleb insisted on
being given the challenge he had longed for since he was forty
years old and he and the other eleven men were sent by Moses
to spy the land of Canaan (Num. 13). At that time, ten of
them brought a bad report that caused the people to fear and
rebel against the Lord. Caleb and Joshua, even though they
acknowledged the strength of the opposition, insisted that the
Israelites could take the land (Num. 13:6–9). Now at an old
age of eighty-five, Caleb picked up the challenge and asked for
the hill country that scared the other spies. God had promised
the land to him forty-five years ago, and that was all he cared
about. "I am still as strong today as the day Moses sent me out;
I am just as vigorous to go out to battle now as I was then.
Now give me this hill country that the Lord promised me that
day ... the Lord helping me, I will drive them out just as He
said" (Josh. 14:11–12).

What caused this man to be so confident in the Lord's
promise to him? His *convictions!* (Josh. 14:7). Caleb had a set

of beliefs about God that convinced him of His faithfulness, so regardless of the formidable challenges and opposition that stood in his way, he was not moved or discouraged. He was completely convinced that God would do what He had promised to do, and that was enough for him. That is what we all need as people of faith in Christ: a set of convictions about our God that will drive our lives for His glory.

Caleb had seen the mighty hand of God that delivered Israel from Egypt (Ex. 7–12). He had witnessed the parting of the Red Sea and the drowning of Pharaoh and the best of his charioteers (Ex. 14:21–30); the bitter waters turned sweet (Ex. 15:22–26); manna from heaven to feed them (Ex. 16); water out of the rock to give them drink (Ex. 17:1–7); and the defeat of the Amalekites as Moses' hand was raised to the Lord (Ex. 17:8–16). Caleb had seen all these mighty works of God and was convinced that He is able to do all things. God is faithful to His promises, and all He asks is for us to trust and obey Him. These were Caleb's convictions. They had become a body of truth that formed the basis of his faith in God.

We too have been given all the evidence we need to know about this mighty God (Rom. 1:18–20). It is the body of truth entrusted to us to keep and walk by (1 Tim. 4:6; Jude 3). If we are to live victoriously in the new life in Christ Jesus, we must have our personal convictions about Him as our great God and Savior.

Who is He to you? What are your convictions about Him? If your convictions about God are as strong as that of Caleb, there is no obstacle that can stand against you in life. You can scale every mountain to possess your inheritance as Caleb did. You can stand against every temptation and overcome in Jesus' name. You can patiently wait for Him when time seems to be running against His coming into your situation. You can persevere in faith when all odds are against you and there seems to be no way to victory. Your convictions about Christ are what will dictate what you will or will not do in such situations, just as the three Hebrew boys affirmed before King Nebuchadnezzar:

> King Nebuchadnezzar, we do not need to defend ourselves before you in this matter. If we are thrown into the blazing furnace, the God we serve is able to deliver us from it, and he will deliver us from Your Majesty's hand. But even if he does not, we want you to know, Your Majesty that we will not serve your gods or worship the image of gold you have set up.
> —Daniel 3:16–18

How about you? Do you have such strong convictions to keep you firmly grounded in Christ and to withstand any shaking and attempt to get you to compromise your faith in Him?

For Reflection

> Then Nebuchadnezzar was furious with Shadrach,
> Meshach and Abednego, and his attitude toward
> them changed. He ordered the furnace heated
> seven times hotter than usual and commanded
> some of the strongest soldiers in his army to
> tie up Shadrach, Meshach and Abednego
> and throw them into the blazing furnace.
> —Daniel 3:19–20

Prayer

Lord, help me to stand firm against the philosophies
of this world and the wisdom of our time that seek
to exalt the self rather than Jesus Christ as Lord.
May I know whom I have believed and be fully
convinced of the veracity of His Word and His
power over everything, seen and unseen. Then I
will not be tossed around and blown here and there
by every wind of doctrine and by the cunning and
craftiness of men in their deceitful scheming. Amen!

3

Pierced by Greed

Those who want to get rich fall into temptation and
a trap and into many foolish and harmful desires
that plunge people into ruin and destruction.
—1Timothy 6:9

H IS FACE LIT with excitement, and a smile swept across his
face as he sat listening intently to his college friends talk
about their country's economic prospects. He had just arrived
for a visit from the United States after a four-year stay and was
reminiscing with his friends. His friends seemed to have made it.
They lived in houses, had their own businesses, and owned their
own cars. People around them fell prostrate in their service for a
morsel of bread. All that incited a yearning in our *been-to* (an old
term for an African who had been to the white man's country and
returned) friend from the United States.

One of his friends made a statement that made his head spin.
The friend casually said in a conversation, "If anybody does not
do everything to acquire wealth in this "rush for gold" going
on in the country now, his children would rise in the future to
condemn him." That was it! The seed had been sown. The net
had been cast and pulled up all the greed in his heart to torment
him. The love of money came dancing before him, and he could
see himself swimming in a pool of wealth filled with recognition
and attention.

So when our friend returned to his foreign home, he closed
the door to every opportunity, quit graduate school, and bundled
his wife and children on a flight back to his home country. He had

no specific plan to pursue and only his foolish shadow, prompted by one casual statement from a friend, to run with.

The story is long, but the lesson that needs to be communicated is that those who want to get rich fall into temptation and a trap and into many foolish and harmful desires that plunge people into ruin and destruction. "For the love of money is a root of all kinds of evil" (1 Tim. 6:9–10). Our been-to friend prospered at a mediocre level in business. He never made those "riches," and the recognition and attention he sought eluded him. Many foolish things came his way, and he almost lost his dignity, but for the timely intervention of God almighty, through the conquering power of the cross of Calvary. Only the grace of God has made this been-to friend of ours your pastor and communicator of that grace.

You see, greed is in the bowels of all mankind. It is that which brought our great, great, great grandparents, Adam and Eve, on their knees before Satan and birthed the sin disease we all inherited from them. It is that which has ruled in the hearts of priests and prophets and the ordinary person in the streets and that which has ruled the hearts of kings and commoners alike. It has ruined kingdoms and imploded vast empires. It manifests in many forms and in many ways. Pastors, deacons, and popes will fight back if you dare call them covetous. But we all are.

So why don't you see greed for what it is and how it may be manifesting in your life and causing the havoc you may be attributing to something else? You see, that's the danger and deceitfulness of greed. It takes the color of your environment and takes cover very well like a chameleon. You can only uncover it when you allow the Spirit of God to shed His light on it. Look for its symptoms in covetousness, lack of satisfaction or contentment, hoarding, lack of generosity, desire for power and more of it, struggle for position and recognition, and even seeking revenge.

It knows no friend or foe, and it does not discriminate. Look out for it, and be wise!

I have been there and testify to the cruelty of its friendliness. Sounds contradictory? Get under the umbrella of "godliness with contentment" (1 Tim. 6:6). You will see and regret the ugliness of the deceit that has ruled your life for years and has pretended to be your best friend for so long.

The grace of God be with you!

For Reflection

Gehazi, the servant of Elisha the man of God, said
to himself, "My master was too easy on Naaman,
this Aramean, by not accepting from him what
he brought. As surely as the LORD lives, I will
run after him and get something from him."
—2 Kings 5:20

Prayer

I am tired of running around for silver and gold,
mansions and cars, and positions and power,
when they never satisfy. Lord, help me to know
Your contentment and be blessed with the peace
that only Your presence can afford. Amen!

4

Integrity Check

Be careful not to do your righteousness
before men, to be seen by them.
—Matthew 6:1

I HAVE OBSERVED THAT so many people are doing very good
things for the wrong reasons. They may mean well, care, and
love much, but it is all done for the wrong reasons. When shaken
to the core, their motives will be faulted. Even though their
actions may benefit or bring relief for many, they have no eternal
consequences. Motive is everything when it comes down to what
pleases God. It is the foundation upon which integrity stands.
For one can do all the right things, but if the motive is wrong, it
means nothing to God, in spite of the loud applause and many
awards society may accord the person. There is a name for it. It is
called hypocrisy, the lack of integrity.

Consider Charlie. He was struggling to buy books for his two
children, and school was reopening in a couple of weeks. He did
not have money for their school fees either, and on top of it all, he
was late on his rent by two months. Had it not been for the timely
intervention of Mr. Chris Afram, his family would have been
thrown out of their house one Tuesday morning. Yet on that same
day, Charlie had sent money to his sister for her child's school
uniform. A special cloth had been designated for the funeral of
their next-door neighbor in the village, so Charlie added some
money for that. The week before the funeral, he went to the local
moneylender and took a loan up to three quarters of his monthly
salary. His buddy, Jack, also needed a loan but was unemployed.

Charlie guaranteed one for him. At the funeral, Charlie donated a handsome amount that was announced with much eloquence by his sister. It brought him much applause and handshakes that made him feel good. Yet he had no peace within because of his neglected obligations at home and the dread of the moneylender's call at the end of the month. Why did he do it, and what did he expect to gain from all of that?

They claim it is an obligation, a requirement, a "have to," a tradition, a love for a sibling and friend, and being a generous giver. It is all public-dependent behavior. Let everybody look away from him, or take out what people will say and you will have a different Charlie.

Jesus has a stern warning for Charlie and company.

> Be careful not to do your righteousness
> before men, to be seen by them.
> —Matthew 6:1

He called such acts hypocrisy. He condemned them in our giving (v. 2), praying (v. 5), and fasting (v. 16). It goes on in our churches, workplaces, and even our most sincere expressions of love for others. Our acts may be good but our motives for doing them may be all wrong. But remember that in the kingdom of God, the end does not justify the means. The means matter more to Him than the end.

Make no mistake about this. Only the things that we do out of love for Jesus have integrity, glorify God, and bring us eternal reward.

> And whatever you do, whether in word or
> deed, do it all in the name of the Lord Jesus.
> —Colossians 3:17

A person who lives this way says and does the same thing whether people are watching or not has integrity. How do you measure?

For Reflection

"You have not cheated or oppressed us," they replied. "You have not taken anything from anyone's hand."
—1 Samuel 12:4

Finally these men said, "We will never find any basis for charges against this man Daniel unless it has something to do with the law of his God."
—Daniel 6:5

Prayer

Lord, strengthen me to be diligent in matters concerning You and to give myself wholly to Your kingdom and its righteousness for Your name's sake. When my integrity is tested and shaken to the core, may I never be found wanting. Let me stand tall above failure and defeat, in the powerful and matchless name of Jesus, amen!

5

Aspire to Be Noble in Character

Now the Berean Jews were of more noble
character than those in Thessalonica,
for they received the message with great
eagerness and examined the Scriptures every
day to see if what Paul said was true.
—Acts 17:11

WHY HAVE WE opened ourselves to the deceit and craftiness
of the Enemy so much these days? Why do we take
delight in disappointments, failure, and losses by the way we treat
Scripture and receive messages supposed to be from God? Why
do we invite and embrace heartache, because we fail to check the
validity of the messages we receive day in and day out?

To protect ourselves from being deceived and disappointed,
one would think that Christians would be curious to know
the source of every word we receive in the name of the Lord,
which is critical for its authentication and scriptural validation.
Unfortunately, we believe everything we are told and move on them
with vigor without validating the source. We have moved blindly
into situations and even enjoyed them, until Mr. Disclaimer walks
in from the supposed source to ruin the party for us.

The modern press is spewing tons of information into our
domain these days without the basic journalistic courtesy of
checking the sources and validating the truth before going to the
press. Yet we too have not taken the time to check their sources
before swallowing what they throw at us. No wonder there is so
much chaos around and everything is falling apart, as the center

gives way, just as the late Nigerian novelist Chinua Achebe put it. We do the same with what we read every day from books and magazines and hear from the people around us. But the worst of it all is how we shamefully treat what we hear from our pulpits and read from the countless books and commentaries coming out these days. Do we stop to check their sources? Don't we fail to check whether they are in conformity with the written Word?

Take a very good and informed look around you and see the countless prophetic ministries springing up every day and how popular they have become. Ask yourself why so many preachers are calling themselves "prophets" these days. Is it not because we have become too lazy to check the source of their message? No wonder the Enemy loves and is laughing to the bank over our itching ears and our lazy and careless manner of treating prophecy. God, help us!

That is why it is so instructive to note that Zerubbabel, the governor, Joshua, the high priest, and "the whole remnant of the people obeyed the voice of the Lord their God, and the message of the prophet Haggai, *because the Lord their God had sent him*" (Hag. 1:12; emphasis mine). It is why when the Spirit of God calls the Jewish congregation in Berea noble that we have to stop and think about it. It is all because the source of what you hear is important for the simple reason of knowing the truth, which alone can set you free, and assuring yourself that you have heard from the Lord so you are standing on solid ground.

I pray, therefore, that you will begin to care more and pay attention to the source of messages you hear in the coming year and make time to review them in the light of God's written Word, for the sound of the message and the oratory of the preacher are not the Word! And I pray also with Paul that "the eyes of your heart may be enlightened" (Eph. 1:18) in order that you may understand what you hear and to know whether it is from God or not before you believe and give yourself away to it.

For Reflection

Then Zerubbabel son of Shealtiel, Joshua son
of Jozadak, the high priest, and the whole
remnant of the people obeyed the voice of the
LORD their God and the message of the prophet
Haggai, because the LORD their God had sent
him. And the people feared the LORD.

—Haggai 1:12)

Prayer

Dear God, please help me to discern the source
of every word or message I hear and to know
whether it comes from You for my edification.
May I be as noble as the congregation of
Berea, making time to seek the veracity
of it from Your eternal Word, amen!

6

Rejoicing at the Misfortune of Others

You should not gloat over your brother in the
day of his misfortune, nor rejoice over the people
of Judah in the day of their destruction, nor
boast so much in the day of their trouble.
—Obadiah 1:12

ONE OF THE greatest tragedies in the church is how much we rejoice over the misfortune of a brother or sister, particularly when we dislike that person for whatever reason. What makes it most wicked is that we pretend to be praying for that person while we gloat over his demise. It is so sickening to hear how people present such situations as prayer topics: the mockery in their tone and the joy you can discern in their faces. May God help us!

Esau was the twin brother of Jacob (Gen. 25:21–26). Because Jacob deceptively received their father's blessings for the first born (27:1–41), there was enmity between the two brothers that spilled over and down through their descendants over the years. When Israel, the nation that descended from Jacob, was brutally overthrown and carried into exile by wicked Assyria, the Edomites, descendants of Esau, stood aloof and rejoiced. They even helped in destroying them (Obad. 8–14). Even though Israel's destruction was judgment from God for their wickedness and idolatry, its brother had no business rejoicing over its demise. That is why God rebuked them so harshly and promised that what they had done would be done to them (v. 15).

God does not rejoice at the misfortune of the sinner. His heart grieves and waits for every sinner to come to repentance and be saved (2 Peter 3:9). Read the prophets and feel God's heart for His rebellious children, knowing where their rebellion would take them and the misfortune it would bring upon them. Therefore, God rebukes them gently and waits patiently for a change of heart and consequent deliverance. That's the expectation of our Lord from all His children. God wants His children to "carry each other's burden" (Gal. 6:2), to be concerned for each other and feel weak when one is weak, and inwardly burn when another is led into sin (2 Cor. 11:28–29). He wants us to confess our sins to each other and pray for each other (James 5:16). That's why the Lord rebuked the Edomites for their attitude when Judah was swept into exile by the Babylonians. "You should not wait at the crossroads to cut down their fugitives, nor hand over their survivors in the day of their trouble" (Obad. 14). After all, we are not like the Philistines who celebrated at the demise of Samson and came under God's judgment (Judg. 16:23–30).

May the Lord give you a heart of repentance and mercy, so that you can feel the pain of your Christian brothers and sisters who may be suffering for a particular sin or disobedience? And may you not gloat over them but be burdened enough to rise in intercessory prayer for them until you see God move in their lives for His greater glory!

For Reflection

Brothers and sisters, my heart's desire and prayer to
God for the Israelites is that they may be saved.
—Romans 10:1

Prayer

Lord, help my heart to bleed for the lost and
the erring that I may stand in the gap for
them until You save and restore them to good
fellowship in Christ. As Your heart and patience
wait for all to come to repentance, may I be
Your instrument to carry Your message of
salvation to them, wherever they may be.

CHAPTER 8

Fruit of the Spirit

1

I Am Love

And so we know and rely on the love God
has for us. God is love. Whoever lives in
love lives in God, and God in them.

—1 John 4:16

I ONCE STOOD on the slippery road of life where no brakes
could hold. My life was a mess and I needed someone to rescue
me. That was my heart's cry, but nobody heard it. To some, I was
all right. To others, I was a jerk who deserved no pity. The clock
of life was ticking fast on me, and I needed someone to hold and
help turn me around.

That was when I met this man. He had been looking at me
for a very long time, waiting to get my attention. When I finally
gave him the opportunity to talk with me, he proved to be a good
listener. He had *patiently* waited for me as I tried hard to ruin my
life. He spoke *kind* words to me, and I felt their warm embrace. It
was like nothing I had experienced before and was very refreshing.
Even though I had somewhere to go, I could not tear myself from
this man's presence. I was captivated.

Then he told me about himself. He is the second person in a family of three called the Godhead. They are the richest family in the entire universe, with no equal in nature and power and authority. His elder brother has control over everything in the family, yet he does *not envy* him. He is thankful and content with what he has, and I could sense the joy in his heart. That was something I was missing in my life, and I knew it. He was *not boastful* about his family wealth and power, and I sensed no *pride* about him. He was simple and effacing.

He offered to help me, but somehow, I thought he had some hidden agenda. I answered him in a sharp and rude manner, but to my shame, he was *not rude* in his response. Rather, he was calm and composed about it. That's when I knew I was talking with the most extraordinary person in the world, a man who was *not self-seeking* or *easily angered*. I felt my heart melt before this stranger, the like of whom I had never met before, so we became friends.

In my crude and impolite manner of speaking, I offended him many times, so I kept apologizing and asking for forgiveness. In every one of those times, he never mentioned the past. That amazed me, so I asked him about it. He told me he kept *no record of my wrongs*. All he wanted me to know was that he *did not delight in evil* ways and that if our friendship was going to deepen on a daily basis as he wants it to, I would have to make a determined and disciplined effort to move away from them. He expects *the truth* at all times, for that brings him great joy.

From that time on, I was sold. There was no way I could let this man go. He was all I ever needed, and I felt life's warmth embracing me again, as hope for the future returned to me.

It's been quite some time since we first met, but I have never asked him his name. All I know is that he has been *always protective* of me. He has been *always trusting* and *always hopeful* in me in spite of my numerous failures. He has never given up on me but has *always persevered* in our strange relationship. So today, I determined to know his name. He smiled and said in a soft and gentle voice, "I *am* love." He is my best friend and everything in this world.

Do you need such a friend in your life? You can find him only in Jesus. The amazing thing is that He has been waiting for you as He patiently waited for me to come to Him and be blessed with eternal life (John 3:16; 1 John 4:8– 10; John 1:12, 13; Rom. 10:9, 10). Will you say yes to Jesus today?

For Reflection

For God so loved the world that he gave his
one and only Son, that whoever believes in
him shall not perish but have eternal life.
—John 3:16

Prayer
Lord Jesus, come into my life this minute and
wash away my sins in Your blood. Transform me
and let me know what real love is, so that I can
love others as You have loved me. I thank You
and pray this in Your precious name, amen!

2

Mrs. Patience

A man's wisdom gives him patience; it
is his glory to overlook an offense.
—Proverbs 19:11

T HE ASHANTIS OF Ghana have a proverb that literally means,
"If you patiently dissect an ant, you will be able to see its
intestines." That says a lot about a character trait in the fruit of
the Spirit called patience.

In this self-centered, fast-paced world, patience is a lost
character trait. We are traveling so fast on the road of technology,
modernization, and prosperity that we cannot wait for anyone
or anything. It is all fast this, fast that. We cannot endure delay,
for it is always now or never. When provoked, our most frequent
response is "I will show you where power lies." Our egos get hurt,
and we quickly get upset and annoyed. We do not persevere
enough when the going gets tough, and we quit so easily. "I
cannot take it anymore," we say, so we seek short-term solutions
that usually lead to a sad and ugly end.

Consider the following episode involving Mrs. Poks, a
maturing Christian.

She sat at the doctor's office, reading a magazine while she
waited for her turn to see the oncologist. Her appointment was
at five o'clock in the evening, but Mrs. Poks had come in very
early to avoid the evening rush. She greeted the receptionist,
announced her appointment time, and then took her seat directly
opposite her. Digging through a neat pile of old magazines, she
found one with an article on a recent research finding on some

fruits that can prevent cancer. It grabbed her attention. When she raised her head from the magazine at last, everybody was gone except two other patients. Shocked at how fast the time had whisked by, she quietly walked to the receptionist and asked why she had not been called to see the doctor at her appointed time. "Madam, the way you were lost in that magazine, I thought reading was more important to you than your appointment with the doctor. I did not want to disturb you. You will have to wait until the next two patients go in before you can see the doctor," the young lady responded rudely. Mrs. Poks couldn't tell what her problem was, but come to think of it, she might have had a very rough night or encounter with a husband or boyfriend. Who knows?

Mrs. Poks could not believe her ears, as a Brit might say. Her mouth dropped as she turned to take her seat. She tried to say something, but she couldn't bring the words out of her mouth. As she took her seat, the two remaining patients offered to cede their turns to her, but she politely declined. A little after half past nine, the receptionist looked up from her tiny glasses and tersely asked, "Are you ready to see the doctor, madam?" Without a word, Mrs. Poks calmly picked up her handbag and walked into the examination room. What an exceptional lady! You can call her Mrs. Patience. (How would you have reacted in that situation?)

At that very moment, a package was delivered to the doctor's office. It contained the long-awaited results of Mrs. Poks' tissue examination, which was critical for her visit that day. The result was negative. The growth in her breast was not cancerous. It was the most refreshing news to hear that evening, and she needed it. Two hours earlier, she would have been asked by the doctor to come back the following day or two because her results were not in.

You see the benefit of patience?

This story may seem ridiculous to some who may think it is impossible for anyone to be that gracious when confronted with such provocation. But that is the difference patience, a fruit of the Spirit, can make in a believer's life. The world would call Mrs. Poks weak and foolish, but in the language of the Bible, she is called a wise woman. "A man's wisdom gives him patience; it is his glory to overlook an offense" (Prov. 19:11). It shapes the character of the believer (Rom. 5:3, 4; James 1:2–5) and glorifies God.

On the other hand, not allowing the Holy Spirit to bear this fruit in your life could prove disastrous, as in the case of King Saul in 1 Samuel 13:8–14. But are you willing to be a "fool" for Jesus?

For Reflection

"What have you done?" asked Samuel ... You have acted foolishly," Samuel said. "You have not kept the command the Lord your God gave you; if you had He would have established you're your kingdom over Israel for all time. But now your kingdom will not endure; the LORD has sought out a man after his own heart and appointed him ruler of his people, because you have not kept the LORD's command."
—1 Samuel 13:11, 13-14

The end of a matter is better than its beginning, and patience is better than pride.
— Ecclesiastes 7:8

Prayer

Lord, help me to be quick to hear but slow
to speak and slow to be angry. I need to be
patient in affliction and in prayer, so that I
can wait for Your responses and timing. I
thank You for answering prayer, amen!

3

Kindness

The islanders showed us unusual kindness.
They built a fire and welcomed us all
because it was raining and cold.
—Acts 28:2

H AVE YOU MET the like of a man who grew up in a large
family in a tough and heartless community? He struggled
to get his share of food when he was growing up. He was shouted
down by his big brothers, asked to do every menial task around
the house, and blamed for everything that went wrong. The
neighborhood was no different. Thugs ruled. One had to be strong
and mean to survive. Age did not matter when it came to doing
things. Everybody was considered equal to every task, and one
either got it done or got shoved around and rolled over. He got
no breaks from anyone and had to fight hard to keep himself in
that community. Now this man grew up and, somehow, got a top
managerial position. He behaved as if he was still in his family
environment and neighborhood. He gave no one any breaks.
He was mean and hard and very difficult to work with. His
inconsiderate and uncaring nature earned him a nickname—
"Terror"—among his workers.

Such is the natural tendency of a man who does not know the
tenderness and kindness of God in Christ Jesus. The world is full
of them. Their environment shapes them, and even though they
hated the hard conditions of their upbringing, they grow to do the
same things to others, or even worse. Statistics show that abusive
children grow up to be equally abusive or more. Maybe that is

why there is so much abuse in the world today. The situation is so bad that even the places that are supposed to be sanctuaries for abused children have become more abusive than the homes they are "rescued" from. People who are trusted with the responsibility of showing love and kindness to abused children have become their worst offenders. That is the ugly nature of sin, but it was not meant to be that way.

God, who made the heavens and the earth, is loving and kind. When He created man, He made him in His own image and likeness (Gen. 1:27). Therefore, man was made to be kind in character. Wickedness and cruelty were not part of His perfect creation, and definitely were not part of His plan for mankind. It is all the result of the fall of man in the garden of Eden (3:6). In spite of that, God acts toward man out of His divine kindness. It is His signature inscribed over all of His creation so He cannot act any other way. Paul testified to this in Acts 14:16, 17, when he said, "In the past, [God] let all nations go their own way. Yet, He has not left Himself without testimony: He has shown kindness by giving you rain from heaven and crops in their seasons; He provides you with plenty of food and fills your hearts with joy."

Even though we are unworthy because of sin, God is still kind to us. That was Jacob's testimony in Genesis 32:10. "I am unworthy of all the kindness and faithfulness you have shown your servant. I had only my staff when I crossed this Jordan, but now I have become two groups."

The ultimate expression of God's kindness to us is in Christ Jesus, through whom He has poured His incomparable riches of grace on us in salvation. "It is by grace you have been saved, through faith—and this not of yourselves, it is the gift of God— not by works, so that no one can boast" (Eph. 2:7–9). He did not just save us; He has equipped us with the ability to be kind to others. This ability comes from His Holy Spirit, who bears His fruit of kindness in those who are yielded to Him (Gal. 5:22).

Therefore, as God's chosen people, we should be able to show compassion and kindness to others (Col. 3:12). It is the right way to commend ourselves to the world (2 Cor. 6:6). We can do this through our speech, in giving, in favor, in practical acts of love, in rebuke, in teaching, in direction, and in guidance, and even in prayer. This cruel world needs a heavy dose of kindness, and we Christians cannot fail our Savior in this venture. He is counting on us.

So will you determine to be kind to someone this week and glorify your Savior?

For Reflection

David asked, "Is there no one still alive
from the house of Saul to whom I can show
God's kindness for Jonathan's sake?"
—2 Samuel 9:1

Prayer

You, oh Lord, are majestic and kind. You show
Your faithfulness and kindness to us in so many
ways, and they open Your heart to us when we
least expect it because of our sins. As You have
been gracious to me, may I also have compassion
for those around me and the tenderness to be
kind even when I am offended. For that is Your
greatest act of kindness to me in Christ Jesus!
It is all for Your witness and glory, amen!

4

Gentleness

Always be prepared to give an answer to everyone
who asks you to give the reason for the hope that
you have. But do this with gentleness and respect,
keeping a clear conscience, so that those who
speak maliciously against your good behavior
in Christ may be ashamed of their slander.

—1 Peter 3:15-16

H AVE YOU BEEN around a person who throws his weight
around and is always in your face? It could be in a group
discussion or one on one with a coworker. Such a person may
be knowledgeable and smart. He may have an answer to every
question and an opinion on every situation, but he doesn't wait
to be asked. He jumps into a discussion and cuts off others who
may be expressing their opinions in a very rude manner. Such a
person is annoying and the person you least want to be around.

Unfortunately, that is the spirit of today: "Be assertive." "Do
not let anybody walk over you." "Tell them your piece of mind."
"If you don't talk harshly, they will not respect you." It is the "me"
world where a person is considered ancient if he has a quiet and
gentle disposition. Such a person is considered weak and a coward.
However, gentleness is not weakness or cowardice. It is strength
under control. It is the right use of authority.

A gentle person is one who knows who he is. He is content
with himself and does not need any externals to assure him of
that. He does not throw his weight around or insist on his rights
in everything. Nor does he trample on others to secure his own.

He gives room for others to express themselves and to even go ahead of him. It does not mean, in such instances, that he has surrendered his rights. He simply respects the rights of others and gives them the opportunity to be heard. When he speaks, he does so at the right time and with the right tone, mindful of the fact that his words can build or break others. He does not allow little insults to irritate him, nor is he disturbed by inconveniences. He holds his own under such trying circumstances. When accused or persecuted, he restrains himself, hopeful of his eventual vindication.

Such is the work the Holy Spirit does in the believer who submits to Him (Gal. 5:23). Without His influence, our selfishness takes over and we run over each other. Moses was a man like that until God brought him under His influence (Ex. 2:11–13). Later, the Bible describes him as the meekest man on the face of the earth (Num. 12:3). When Aaron and Miriam spoke against him, he did not retaliate or assert himself as the boss. He gave room for God to address the situation in His own way (4–15). Because of his gentleness, he was able to lead a very stubborn people for forty years in the wilderness.

Jesus is the epitome of gentleness. That's why He calls on all who are weary and burdened to come to Him and find rest for their souls (Matt. 11:28–30). His gentleness was evident throughout His earthly ministry. Even though He was God, He did not assert Himself as God but became a servant, learned obedience, and in humility, went to the cross for our sins (Phil. 2:5–11). He brought His power under the control of the Father while on earth.

When we allow the Holy Spirit to take control of all our thoughts and emotions, we too become gentle and humble at heart like Him. The world may take us to be fools, but that is God's wisdom and power at work in us.

For Reflection

But the fruit of the Spirit is love, joy,
peace, patience, kindness, goodness,
faithfulness, gentleness and self-control.
—Galatians 5:22–23

Prayer

I submit to You, Lord Holy Spirit. Bear Your fruit
of gentleness in me, so that I may be able to bear
with others and live like Jesus, our gentle Savior.

CHAPTER 9

Spiritual Gifts

1

Hospitality

Offer hospitality to one another without grumbling.
—1 Peter 4:9

THEY HAD MET him for the first time and did not know anything about him. The small man just sat down with his small entourage close to the women who had gathered by a riverside and eavesdropped for a few minutes. He was bald and a little heavyset. His appearance revealed the haste in which he had left wherever he had come from, and one could easily discern that he was new to the area and lost. Yet he had the audacity to cut into their conversation with some short comments now and then. His comments were concise and too revealing to ignore. Whoever he was, there was no doubt that this short man was an authority on the subject the ladies were discussing. But they wanted to mind their own business, so the five ladies continued their discussion until they were ready to leave. That was when this stranger picked up the tail and asked if he could pray for them. The prayer was so electrifying that the whole atmosphere changed. They had been in this riverside meeting many times and had encountered men who had rudely interrupted their conversation before, but this short man was different.

Paul formerly greeted the ladies after the prayer and introduced himself and his associates: Dr. Luke, Silas, and Timothy. They had come to Philippi because Paul had heard a distress call from a man in his dream one night, and taking it to be God's leading, they sailed the next morning and arrived in Philippi, where they met the women at the riverside (Acts 16:6-15).

Lydia, one of the ladies, got very curious and inquired after their message with great anticipation. Paul cleared his throat and began his discourse on Christ Jesus and new covenant in His blood. It was the moment he had been waiting for, and he did not disappoint. In the end, the women believed and were baptized. Lydia, knowing that the men were strangers to their city, urged them to come and stay in her house. "If you consider me a believer in the Lord," she said, "come and stay at my house" (v. 15).

What a day that had been! Both parties had gone to the riverside for different reasons, but God had planned something different for them. He is the God who sees into the future and provides for our needs (Gen. 22:14), for in their meeting, God had met Lydia's deepest need—salvation—and Paul's prayer before he had even uttered them. Paul did not know that Lydia was God's appointed host for them, but he gave her the good news and the opportunity to be saved. Lydia also did not know who Paul was—the great apostle to the Gentiles and the great instructor on the Christian faith and the church. She just had a hospitable spirit so she opened her house to them out of gratitude and their need of a place to stay.

Hebrews 13:2 reminds us not to forget to entertain strangers, because it is good and rewarding. Hospitality is making real to others, our spiritual fruit of love, goodness, and kindness (Gal. 5:22–23). When we open our hearts to help others, God answers our own prayers and meets our needs in ways we may not even recognize. So be encouraged by Lydia's example and receive God's blessings today.

It is difficult to know who to trust in our time, but God is able to direct your heart in such circumstances, if you open yourself to hospitality, as Abraham did. You will then receive the blessing of knowing what is in God's heart and what He plans to do concerning you and your family (Gen. 18:1–33).

For Reflection

He said, "If I have found favor in your eyes, my
lord, do not pass your servant by. Let a little water
be brought, and then you may all wash your feet
and rest under this tree. Let me get you something
to eat, so you can be refreshed and then go on your
way—now that you have come to your servant."
—Genesis 18:3–5

Prayer

I open my heart to You, and also my home
and my treasure. Take them, Lord, and use
them to bless whomever You direct me to
welcome and bless with my gifts and resources.
Thank You for this opportunity to bless
and be blessed in Christ Jesus, amen!

2

Encouragement

God heard the boy crying, and the angel of
God called to Hagar from heaven and said to
her, "What is the matter, Hagar? Do not be
afraid; God has heard the boy crying as he lies
there. Lift the boy up and take him by the hand,
for I will make him into a great nation."
—Genesis 21:17–18

NOTHING IN THIS world refreshes the soul more than the
comforting presence of a friend or brother when you really
need it. For in this life, there is always a moment when you find
yourself completely down and out, needing a friendly hand to lift
you up and help you back on your feet. It could be the time when
life finds you at the bottom of your well of affliction or destitution,
that time when nothing is working for you and no one seems to
understand. It could be that period when you have messed up
big time and need the friendly ear of a brother or sister to confess
to, one who will gently and lovingly rebuke you and commit to
stand with you through your repentance and restoration. It could
even be that time when you are stubbornly refusing to accept
your sinfulness and need a true brother or sister to sit you down,
look you straight in your eyes, and let you know straight up that
you are wrong. And it could be that occasion when something
strange has happened in your life or home that has made you the
prime-time topic on Gossip Lane and you need an angel to reveal
some things to you, for you have no clue about what is happening
to you. Or it could be that happy moment of victory in your

life that you cannot share with just anybody and you need that special somebody to share and rejoice with. Such moments are like drinking a glass of cold water on a dry and sunny afternoon.

Imagine how Hagar must have felt when the angel of the Lord opened her eyes to see the well of water in the desert when she was certain that Ishmael would die of thirst (21:14–19). How about Joseph's special moment when Judah pulled him out of the dry cistern (38:26–28) or fugitive Moses when Reuel invited him to stay with him and his family (Ex. 2:18–22)? And then there was Naomi when her husband and two sons died and Ruth committed to stick with her till death (Ruth 1:14–22). There was David in the cave of Adullam, when his family and all the Israelites "who were in distress, or in debt or discontent gathered around him and he became their leader (1 Sam. 22:1, 2). And what about David when the prophet Nathan rebuked him after his adulterous relationship with Bathsheba and the killing of Uriah, her husband (12:1–14)? How about Mephibosheth, the crippled son of Jonathan, when David invited him to dine at his table (9:1–13)? And finally, there was the adulterous woman the crowd wanted to stone, until Jesus' timely intervention (John 8:1–11).

Then there was Elizabeth when Mary visited her. She was pregnant with John in her old age and had been in seclusion for five months (Luke 1:24). Mary too had received the news from angel Gabriel that she would carry and give birth to the Messiah, even though she was a virgin (26–35). The two women needed each other in their extraordinary moments of joy, and they shared three months in Elizabeth's home encouraging each other. What a picture of grace!

Somewhere around you today, there may be a Hagar, Joseph, Moses, Naomi, David, Mephibosheth, Elizabeth, or Mary who needs your encouraging word or presence to see him through his moment of trial or joy. Can you allow yourself to be God's instrument of encouragement to that person? Or maybe you are the one needing that encouragement. May the Lord send someone your way today, and may you rejoice in His gracious presence today!

For Reflection

But Barnabas took him and brought him to the apostles. He told them how Saul on his journey had seen the Lord and that the Lord had spoken to him, and how in Damascus he had preached fearlessly in the name of Jesus.

—Acts 9:27

For I was hungry and you gave me something to eat, I was thirsty and you gave me something to drink, I was a stranger and you invited me in, I needed clothes and you clothed me, I was sick and you looked after me, I was in prison and you came to visit me.

—Matthew 25:35–37

Prayer

Lord, make me an instrument of warmth and of comfort to someone who is in dire need of Your support and encouragement. Fill my heart with joy as You use me to refresh others, amen!

Chapter 10

Discernment

1

Missteps in Life

> When a gentle south wind began to blow, they
> saw their opportunity; so they weighed anchor
> and sailed along the shore of Crete. Before
> very long, a wind of hurricane force, called the
> Northeaster, swept down from the island.
> —Acts 27:13–14

Some time ago, I went to the dentist with my son after we had dropped off my daughter at work. I mapped the drive back home in my mind, and with the route I had planned to take, I expected to be home within fifteen minutes. Traffic was good, and as I drove without a stop or slow down, I congratulated myself for my navigational expertise on the roads of Dakar. We came to the point where I had to go around to my right, merge into the overpass traffic, and continue onto the Auto Route. I looked straight ahead and saw Route de Rufisque, which was closer to my house, and unusually clear of traffic, so I decided to go that way.

For a few minutes, the route was fine. However, when we ran into the heavy industrial traffic that was characteristic of that road, I knew I had made a terrible misjudgment. As we sat in that crawling, sweltering Tuesday morning traffic for about forty-five minutes, I kept asking my son, "Why did I come this way?" I am sure he answered in his head, "Because you are a fool." But that's not something a son can say to his dad, so he wisely refused to suggest any answer. Then I heard the voice of the Lord saying, "That's how life is. One misstep and you will be subjected to unnecessary delays, discomfort, frustrations, regrets, and all the negatives you can think of. You will go winding and running around for a long time when you could have made it in a very short time, if you had kept your head straight and stuck to your original, well-thought-out plan." I sensed strongly that it was a lesson for my son, who had just graduated from high school and was preparing to step out into the world and college life. So we talked about it.

Life is a journey, and everyone who undertakes it must have a road map and a plan. The road map is provided by the Architect of this world: God almighty. By the guidance of His Holy Spirit, He provides counsel for each traveler to plan his trip to eternity. It takes commitment to Jesus Christ, sensitivity to His Spirit, and obedience to His voice to receive from God and to stay on the right road, which is characteristically narrow (Matt. 7:14). For a challenge, the world provides several appealing alternatives that suit the flesh much better. Any misstep onto that broad road (v. 13), which many are traveling on, could become for you like my experience in this story or that of the Israelites before entering Canaan.

Proverbs 4:23–27 says,

> Above all else, guard your heart, for it is the wellspring of life … Let your eyes look straight ahead … Take only ways that are firm. Do not swerve to the right or the left.

It is very wise counsel from a very wise king who took some very foolish missteps in his life and suffered for them. His words, as the Holy Spirit moved him to write, are worthy of your attention and serious consideration.

For Reflection

When the LORD has fulfilled for my lord every good thing he promised concerning him and has appointed him ruler over Israel, my lord will not have on his conscience the staggering burden of needless bloodshed or of having avenged himself.
—1 Samuel 25:30–31

Prayer

I thank You, Lord, for the counsel of Abigail to David that stopped him from taking a misstep that could have been disastrous for him in the future, just as the issue of Bathsheba became to him. I pray that You will give me discernment and much wisdom into all things before I take any decision and make any move in life. In His precious name, I pray with thanksgiving, amen!

2

Misconceptions

The jailer woke up, and when he saw the
prison doors open, he drew his sword and
was about to kill himself because he thought
the prisoners had escaped. But Paul shouted,
"Don't harm yourself! We are all here!"

—Acts 16:27–28

LITTLE ADWO WAS all smiles that evening. She had just
finished talking with her best friend about school and how
their first day back from vacation was going to be special for her.
For the past five years, her friends had ridiculed her for coming
to school by *tro-tro* (the local minibus system in Ghana) while
they came in their parents' cars. But this school year was going
to be different.

During the summer vacation, her dad, Mr. Pinto, had changed
jobs and, as a result, his financial portfolio had been revised
considerably upward. He therefore bought a brand-new car as a
gift for his wife on her birthday, and Adwo could not wait to have
her mother drive her to school when it reopened; she relished the
reaction of her friends.

On the evening before D-day, Mrs. Pinto sat to braid Adwo's
hair. She was dressed in her beautiful nightgown her husband
had given her as part of her birthday present. With rollers in her
hair, mother and daughter joked about the possible scenarios at
school the following day. Suddenly, the doorbell rang insistently.
When Mrs. Pinto opened the door, Kate, her best friend, pushed
her way into their living room. "I have always told you not to trust

that man. I just saw your husband with another woman in the Emerald Hotel," she reported.

In anger, Mrs. Pinto grabbed her car keys and drove toward the Emerald, leaving little Adwo crying. Not quite five minutes later, a neighbor came running to the house. Mrs. Pinto had driven into a small pillar as she negotiated a curve, and she died instantly. Kate rushed to the Emerald with the aim of "giving it" to Mr. Pinto for causing the untimely death of her best friend. After tipping a bellhop, she was directed to Room 312, so into the elevator and up to the third floor she went. When Kate opened the door, she was shocked at what she saw. Mr. Pinto was in a meeting called by his international director, who had arrived from Zurich that afternoon, with five other coworkers. And the woman she saw was the director.

What a tragedy!

Such stories abound all over the world. People have been profiled in many ways. Some have lost their jobs or promotions, many have been incarcerated, while others have been murdered, all because some people did not take time to know the facts. They saw or heard a piece of the story and drew their conclusions.

In Philippi, Paul and Silas were thrown in jail for delivering a demon-possessed girl (Acts 16:25–34). As they sang at midnight, there was a violent earthquake. Their chains fell off and the doors flew open. The jailer attempted suicide, thinking the prisoners had escaped. Paul told him not to kill himself because they were all there. His misconception of what must have happened, driven by fear, could have ended in a personal and family tragedy, had it not been for Paul's timely intervention.

So before you draw your conclusions about people, or come up with your views on issues, be sure you have all the facts. If you are not sure, do everybody a favor by remaining silent.

It is always better to assess the consequences of your actions, keeping in mind that you could be wrong, before you destroy somebody's life.

To inform you of the end of the Kate saga, Mr. Pinto was never the same again. About two and a half years after her wife's tragic death, he died of hypertension. Little Adwo and her younger brother were orphaned for life because of the misconception of a "friend" of their mother who became her indirect murderer. Things may never be what you think they are at first sight, so let's be careful.

For Reflection

When the south wind blew softly, supposing
that they had obtained their desire, putting out
to sea, they sailed close by Crete. But not long
after, a tempestuous head wind arose, called
Euroclydon. So when the ship was caught, and
could not head into the wind, we let her drive.
—Acts 27:13–15

A faithful witness does not lie,
But a false witness will utter lies.
—Proverbs 14:5

There is a way that seems right to a man,
But its end is the way of death.
—Proverbs 14:12

Prayer

Lord, help me to see and discern right before I open
my mouth about something or to choose a course
of action in life. Let me be a faithful witness and
not one who is eventually found to be a liar. Amen!

3

Lord Give Us Sight

And Elisha prayed, "Open his eyes, LORD, so
that he may see." Then the LORD opened the
servant's eyes, and he looked and saw the hills full
of horses and chariots of fire all around Elisha.

—2 Kings 6:17

THE CALL FINALLY came. Our two guests were arriving at the
Leopold Senghor International Airport at 1:35 am. Looking
at the time, there was no way I could get some sleep and make
it to the airport in time to meet them. Realizing this, I decided
to tackle an assignment I had vowed to finish early this week. So
with our usual cups of tea, I sat in bed by my wife and got busy
on my laptop.

At exactly one o'clock, I drove to the airport and waited,
looking intently for our guests. After searching for an hour and
a half, I found our two guests standing right to my left. How
could I have missed them all this time? It turned out they had
arrived earlier and walked out without seeing me. Thinking they
had missed me, they walked out of the waiting area and tried
to call me. When my wife told them I was at the airport, they
walked back to the waiting area and waited for me. They had been
looking for me and I had been looking for them, but none of us
saw each other until then.

The point I am making here is this: Sometimes, we need the
Lord to open our eyes to see what we have been waiting for, or we
will grow weary and give up. Many times, God's blessings are all
around us. His answers to our prayers have been dispatched to us,

but our minds are clouded with anxiety and many distractions—our preconditions, picture of, and preferences—so we can't see with God. We cry and shout and pray more, thinking God has not heard us. We complain and even become jealous toward others and what they have, yet God's answers are right there before us, waiting to be embraced. But we don't see them. Those are times we have to pray for God to give us spiritual eyes to see. He cares about us so much that He has time to show us little things like a nagging mosquito to kill when we ask Him to show it to us.

That is my favorite story of my wife. She was looking to kill a mosquito that had kept her awake all night but couldn't find it. In her desperation, she prayed and asked the Lord to reveal where that little rascal was hiding. She recounts that, instantly after the prayer, her eyes fell on her tormentor and, with a big bang that would have killed an elephant, crushed that tiny thing to its eternal grave.

Abraham's servant prayed to the Lord to show him the woman He had chosen for Isaac, and the Lord revealed Rebekah according to his request (24:12–27). Jacob's eyes were opened to see the stairway from heaven to the earth with angels ascending and descending at Bethel (28:16). Elisha prayed, and his servant's eyes were opened to see the hills around them filled with horses and chariots of fire (2 Kings 6:17). Isaiah, Mary Magdalene, the disciples after the resurrection, Steven, Paul, and many others have had their eyes opened to see God's glory and His blessings around them.

We too need our eyes to be opened to see His blessings, provision, and protection around us—the husbands and wives we have been waiting for, the jobs and business opportunities staring at us, and the financial and other provisions He has released to us. They are all right in front of us, waiting to be seen and accessed.

That's why we all need to pray, "Lord, give us sight."

For Reflection

Then God opened her eyes and she saw a
well of water. So she went and filled the skin
with water and gave the boy a drink.
—Genesis 21:19

Prayer

Lord, open my eyes to behold Your glory in
Your daily provision, protection, direction,
and many more actions to my family and
me, my community, and Your church.
In the name that is above every name in
heaven, on earth, and in the earth, amen!

CHAPTER 11

Obedience

1

Do We Hear Him When He Speaks?

Then the LORD said to Cain, "Why are you angry?
Why is your face downcast? If you do what is
right, will you not be accepted? But if you do not
do what is right, sin is crouching at your door; it
desires to have you, but you must rule over it."
—Genesis 4:6–7

THERE IS A strong urge in man that drives him to satisfy the
self and ego all the time. It reveals itself in many ways, but no
matter what form and shape it takes, it is the same caricature called
sin nature—or simply, the self. It was inherited from our ancestor,
Adam, in the garden of Eden. It is ugly and manipulative. It adorns
itself in the best apparel and speaks smoothly like melted butter on
freshly baked bread. It is wicked and spares no one, regardless of
race, creed, or stature. It can lift you up to the highest height and
then, when your head is spinning with delight, drop you like lead to
drown in a pool of water. When you are soaring on its wings, high
above cloud nine, or in the gloom that surrounds you, you can hear
no other voice but your own; not even the voice of the Almighty.

Look at what it did to Cain. It made him so sour that he failed to hear God's warning (Gen. 4:4–7). Listen to the people of Noah's day. "Hey, old man, what are you building—a ship?" For one hundred and twenty years, they laughed, scorned, and indulged in revelry until the floods swept them away. Did anybody hear Noah's preaching and warnings (Gen. 6, 7)? Did Moses and Aaron hear God when He told them to speak to the stone at Meribah (Num. 20)? What about Israel's first King? Did Samuel make sense to Saul when God told him to annihilate the Amalekites (1 Sam. 15)?

Fast-forward to the New Testament. Did Peter hear Jesus when He told him that Satan had asked to "sift him as wheat" but that He had prayed for him? (Luke 22:32) Why then did he boast that he would even die for Jesus (33)? How about Martha when her brother Lazarus died? She was disappointed, and perhaps angry, when Jesus showed up four days after Lazarus' death. "*Did Jesus care?* ", she might have thought. At that time, nothing Jesus said made sense to her (John 11:21–27; 39–40). Why couldn't Martha hear Jesus when he spoke? It's all because of the self!

You see, we often hear God through our hurts and disappointments when He fails to be at our beck and call. We want our way and time in everything, but He has other ideas, so we don't see what He is doing in that situation for His own glory and our strengthening. Other times, our stubborn attitudes, prejudiced minds, selfish ambitions, arrogance, wickedness, and bruised pride and egos prevent us from hearing God when He speaks. We hear Him only through the manifestations of the old self—our sinful nature. But if only we could always push the flesh aside and listen through our new nature (1 Cor. 5:17), we would often perceive Him, or "get His drift," as they say. Then we would know that he is truly never late, that in our weak moments, when He seems to be silent, He is really saying, "My grace is sufficient for you, for my strength is made perfect in [your] weakness" (2 Cor. 12).

So can you really hear Jesus today when He says, "I will never leave you or forsake you" (Heb. 13:5)?

For Reflection

Philip said, "Lord, show us the Father and that will be enough for us." Jesus answered: "Don't you know me, Philip, even after I have been among you such a long time? Anyone who has seen me has seen the Father. How can you say, 'Show us the Father'?"
—John 14:8–9

Prayer

Lord Jesus, heal my broken heart and remove my hurts, pains, and disappointments so that I may hear You when You speak. May I never miss Your voice but always discern You in every situation, amen!

CHAPTER 12

Giving

1

Honor Him with Your Wealth

Honor the LORD with your wealth, with
the firstfruits of all your crops.
—Proverbs 3:9

ONE OF THE most difficult things to do in life is to part with
money. The Akans of Ghana say that it is like pulling hair
from your nose. It is awfully painful, and sometimes, it draws
blood. However, before the right grooming tools were invented,
hair pulling was necessary if a person did not want to look like a
rat. Taking care of nose hair was a symbol of honoring one's body.
Likewise, giving at church is one of the most difficult things for
most believers, just like our friend, Kofi.

He had been praying for a job for a long time and most of his
résumés had received no responses. He was a member of his church's
prayer team and had seen many people they prayed for get results.
And that made him angry with God. He decided to walk away
from church for some time and commit more time to job hunting.

One day, Kofi met a man in the house of one of his unbelieving
friends, and as they talked, his situation came up. The bitterness in

his heart that spilled out when he talked about it was unbearable. The man interrupted Kofi's griping with a statement that shocked him. "Christians are a bunch of fair-weather and ungrateful people who show no commitment to the God they profess to love." Kofi quickly tried to justify himself, so he bragged about his devotion to God and His service, both in the church and community. The man said nothing about Kofi's defense but simply asked him to submit his résumé to his office the following day.

As Kofi sat in the man's office the day after his third interview, he could not believe the man's simplicity. He was rich, but his wealth did not go ahead of him. He offered Kofi a job with a comfortable five-figure salary. As they shook hands at the door, the man said to him, "Congratulations, Kofi. But don't forget to honor the Lord with your wealth."

The end of the month came and Kofi got his first paycheck with a smile. At church the following Sunday, the offering bowl came around and Kofi put in the amount he had been giving before the new job, without a tithe or a thanksgiving offering. He had conveniently forgotten the exhortation of his boss when he was hired.

When King Solomon wrote Proverbs 3:9, he was conscious of how difficult and painful it is for many of us to commit our finances to the Lord. He knew that the ability and willingness to do this with joy reveals how much esteem one has for God, who is the giver and owner of it all. It also reveals how detached one is from his wealth and how submissive he is to the Lord. But he noted that it is all for our good, for the benefit of giving to God is an overflowing harvest from your labor (10).

So how is your giving? Do you consider it an act of honor to the Lord? Do you realize that the abundance of your harvest this year depends on how you honor the Lord with your wealth? Have you considered giving a firstfruit offering to the Lord this year?

To know how committed you are to the Lord, check how freely and joyfully you give to Him.

For Reflection

Remember this: Whoever sows sparingly
will also reap sparingly, and whoever sows
generously will also reap generously. Each
of you should give what you have decided in
your heart to give, not reluctantly or under
compulsion, for God loves a cheerful giver.
—2 Corinthians 9:6–7

Prayer

Lord, help me to know how to give to You
with a smile and a cheer in my heart that taps
into Your benevolent grace and abundant
blessings, in the name of Jesus, amen!

CHAPTER 13

Witnessing

1

The Most Appreciated Men

This is a day of good news and we
are keeping it to ourselves.
—1 Kings 7:9

T HEY WERE DESPISED and abandoned. Nobody wanted to be around them because of their skin condition. The law was very specific on what to do with such people. "Put out of camp every leper" (Num. 5:2). And so, to outside the city gates they were banished, quarantined from the community. In fact, their situation was so bad that the law went further to prescribe specific garments for them and instructions on how to relate to other people. "Now, the leper ... his clothes shall be torn and his head bare, and he shall cover his mustache, and cry, 'Unclean! Unclean!' (Lev. 13:45).

That was the situation of the four men at the city gate of Samaria (2 Kings 7:3). The Arameans had laid a long siege to the city. As a result, there was a great famine in the city to the extent that "a donkey's head sold for eighty shekels of silver" (2 Kings 6:25). There was death inside and outside the city, so the four lepers decided to put their lives in the hands of the Aramean army by going into their camp. To their utter surprise, the camp was deserted. God had caused a miracle and the soldiers had run for their lives, leaving behind all their food and property. The lepers "ate and drank and carried away silver, gold and clothes, and went and hid them" (7:8). I wonder what they intended to do with the fine clothes since they couldn't wear them anyway, but that is the natural inclination of the human heart.

Greed has tightened its grip on the hearts of men, and no matter how useless some things may be to us, we still covet them. It is the main cause of corruption and disorder in society today (1 Tim. 6:10). The love of money and property has displaced God from the life of contemporary man and society. However, "we brought nothing into this world, and we will take nothing out of it" (8).

The lepers finally realized they were acting selfishly. "This is a day of good news and we are keeping it to ourselves" (1 Kings 7:9). And so, they went and reported the good news to the gatekeepers, and as a result, the whole city was saved. The most hated people in Samaria became the most appreciated men in town.

We too have been given custody of the best news in the world: the gospel of Christ. God caused a miracle on Calvary, and the sin of the world was washed away in the blood of His Son, Jesus Christ. We were like the lepers at the gate of Samaria, with death within and without. But Jesus conquered death and gave us new life in Himself (Col. 1:13–14). It is good news for the world, and we have to tell others (2 Cor. 5:18–20). Unfortunately, most of us are keeping it to ourselves.

While we rejoice in our salvation, we have forgotten those dying in the world. But like the lepers, we too have to realize that we're not doing the right thing. Let us, therefore, go and proclaim the good news of Christ's redemptive work to a dying world. Then the Word would be true of us that say, "How beautiful are the feet of those who bring good news" (Rom. 10:15).

For Reflection

But if I say, "I will not mention his word or speak anymore in his name," his word is in my heart like a fire, a fire shut up in my bones. I am weary of holding it in; indeed, I cannot.
—Jeremiah 20:9

Prayer

Lord, help me to see the vanity of this world and the faces of people who are lost but do not even see it. May I be burdened with their desperate need for Your saving grace and plead for mercy to birth faith in their heart and bring them home to You, in the precious name of Your Son, Jesus Christ, amen!

2

Would You Have Witnessed to Cornelius?

At Caesarea there was a man named Cornelius,
a centurion in what was known as the Italian
Regiment. He and all his family were devout
and God-fearing; he gave generously to those
in need and prayed to God regularly.

—Acts 10:1–2

W HEN THE CHURCH talks about evangelism, what do we
think about? What is the sphere within which we define
evangelism? Oftentimes, we think about the "people in the world,"
and by that, we mean those who are not attending our Sunday
services and therefore need to be invited to worship with us. But
when we assume that every registered, tithe-paying member of
a local church is heaven bound, we exclude a great number of
people who need to be saved from our evangelism strategies. We
normally forget that a majority of the millions of people who fill
out magnificent edifices called churches are going to hell and need
to be ministered to.

Most often, we look at people and think, *Wow! What wonderful
Christians!* They may be the first in our services on Sundays,
Sunday school, Wednesday Bible studies, and prayer meetings.
They can fast forty days and forty nights. They can pray heaven
down. And to top it all off, they abound in generosity. However,
they do not know the right way of salvation and are hurting,
even though they look and sound all right. Such people are like
Cornelius, the centurion of what was called the Italian Regiment
in Caesarea (Acts 10:1).

Cornelius was "a devout man and one who feared God with his entire household, who gave alms generously to the people, and prayed to God always" (2). Listen to God's own testimony about him: "Your prayers and your alms have come up for a memorial before God" (4b). If God recognized Cornelius that highly, why then did he have to worry about salvation? It's because Cornelius, like everybody else, needed to be born-again (John 1:12, 13). That is the only way one can enter heaven (John 14:6). That's why the angel of God told Cornelius in a vision to "send for Simon whose surname is Peter ... He will tell you what you must do" (6).

Our local churches are filled with millions like Cornelius, "good people" who would go straight to hell if they died today. We sing, pray, fellowship, break bread, and laugh with them every Sunday without sensing the need to talk to them about being born again. This lack of evangelism within the church itself could be the reason why the influence of the church is so weak in the world. But until a person experiences a personal heart change, he cannot influence another person for Christ. And I am not talking about tongue speaking as a sign of being born again. I am talking about true believers who have yielded their hearts to the Spirit of God and the lordship of Christ Jesus and are seeking, above all things, the "Kingdom of God and His righteousness" (Matt.6:33).

So will you begin to open your eyes and allow the Lord to show you the "Cornelius" around you today so that you may be a Peter to that person (Acts 10:34–43)? Do not be bound by traditions in the church (14) or be fooled by what you see about such people (2). Be discerning, hear their heart's cry for salvation, and lead them to Christ.

For Reflection

Not everyone who says to Me, "Lord, Lord," shall
enter the kingdom of heaven, but he who does the
will of My Father in heaven. Many will say to Me
in that day, "Lord, Lord, have we not prophesied
in Your name, cast out demons in Your name,
and done many wonders in Your name?" And
then I will declare to them, "I never knew you;
depart from Me, you who practice lawlessness!"
—Matthew 7:21–23

Prayer

Lord, I cannot see the hearts of men like You can.
As my humanity limits, I can only go by what
I see, but I know that because I have You, I no
longer operate in the natural but the supernatural.
Give me discerning eyes to see the hurting and
unsaved, the love and compassion to care about
their hurt and spiritual state, and the boldness
to share with them the gift of salvation. Amen!

3

Just Tell, and Invite

Philip found Nathanael and told him, "We
have found the one Moses wrote about in
the Law, and about whom the prophets also
wrote—Jesus of Nazareth, the son of Joseph."
—John 1:45

O NE OF THE main hindrances to personal witnessing is fear
that they will not believe our story. We often think that
they will not come anyway, so why bother ourselves? But that is
the lie of the Devil who wants to continue his rule over the lives
of people who have been set free by Christ Jesus on Calvary but
are still living in darkness. All they have to do to receive their
deliverance and salvation is to hear the message, believe, repent,
confess, and submit to the lordship of Christ (Rom. 10:8–10).
Satan knows that it is the work of the Holy Spirit to convict the
sinner of sin and to bring him to repentance. Yet he wants us to
believe that it is our work so we get frustrated when our witness
is rejected. It has become one of the main hindrances to personal
evangelism, and that must change. Maybe the simple witness of
Philip to Nathanael might help to encourage us.

Philip was one of the twelve disciples Jesus appointed as
apostles (Luke 6:12–16). He was personally called to discipleship
by Jesus (John 1:43). After that, Philip went to Nathanael and
told him about Christ, and this was his simple witness: "We
have found the One Moses wrote about whom the prophets also
wrote—Jesus of Nazareth, the son of Joseph" (45). That's it—a
very simple and direct witness, without any theological dialogue.

He had finished his job, and the onus was upon Nathanael to believe or reject his witness. And that's the point.

You see, our responsibility as believers of Jesus Christ is to tell others about Him and His sacrificial offering on Calvary for everyone who will believe (John 3:16). It is as simple as ABCD. Every believer has a witness about Jesus Christ to tell others. What brought you to Christ? How has your life changed since you believed? That, every believer should be able to do. You do not need a degree in advanced theology to convince anyone about Christ. Ours is to just tell, and the rest is in God's hands.

Nathanael pushed back Philip's witness with a question. "Nazareth! Can anything good come from there?" (46a). "Come and see," Philip responded (46b). I love it! Philip did not engage Nathanael in any theological argument to prove his point. Nor did he allow himself to be sucked into any geographical or territorial dispute about goodness or otherwise. All he said was, "Come and see." Simple! It is the simplest invitation to discipleship that anyone can put out. You don't have to get disappointed with their expression of doubt. It's normal, and you should expect it. Just invite them to try Jesus or to come to church. The rest is in His able hands, and that's the beauty of our Lord.

He knows how to deal with everyone. Because He knows everyone before even conception, He knows how to work with each one of us to take the first step of discipleship, and that's what He did with Nathanael. When he took Philip's challenge, and Jesus saw him approaching, He remarked, "Here is a true Israelite, in whom there is nothing false" (47). Nathanael was shocked by that statement, so he asked Jesus how He knew him. The Lord responded, "I saw you while you were still under the Fig tree before Philip called you" (48). That was the nail in the coffin for Nathanael. It blew him away. How could Jesus know him that well? And how could He know where he was before Philip called him? I am sure he said to himself that if this man from Nazareth could know him and all about him, then He was none other than the Messiah.

> "Rabbi, you are the Son of God; you are the
> King of Israel," Nathanael confessed.
> —John 1:49

That's the wonder of our Jesus; that's what He can do to every human heart that takes the first step "to see." But they cannot take that first step if we don't invite them, and that's where Jesus is counting on every one of us.

So may the story of Philip and Nathanael encourage you to take personal responsibility for telling the gospel story and inviting people to come and see for themselves the greatest redemption project ever undertaken in the entire universe; and may the Holy Spirit be your power and strength!

For Reflection

> "Everyone who calls on the name of the Lord will be
> saved" ... And how can they hear without someone
> preaching to them? And how can anyone preach
> unless they are sent? As it is written: "How beautiful
> are the feet of those who bring good news!"
> —Romans 10:13–15

Prayer

Lord, help me to be a witness for You and to live in obedience to Your Great Commission. Take away all shyness and intimidation that often hold me back. And may I move in Your ability and wisdom to simply speak of Your love to all who care to know. Thank You, in Jesus' name. Amen.

4

Ignorance

In the past God spoke to our ancestors through
the prophets at many times and in various ways,
but in these last days he has spoken to us by his
Son, whom he appointed heir of all things, and
through whom also he made the universe.

—Hebrews 1:1–2

WHEN THE WISE say that "ignorance is a disease," it is
true. I have observed that when one ignores learning, one
lacks so much knowledge that one becomes a social misfit and an
incompetent person (or functionally useless person) in many areas
of life. This truth was demonstrated in the funny story of Sarah
at a social dinner with her fiancé's family and friends.

Kwaku's father, Mr. Fosu, organized the dinner at the Hotel
Marina, set on a cliff at the beach, with a breathtaking view of the
city by night. The guests began to arrive around six thirty in the
evening, and by seven, they were all seated. As the proud father-
in-law to be, he went through his introductory speech with much
grace, sprinkled with some good, old-time humor. He then called
for a toast to his son and his fiancé. So to a hearty "Cheers," the
glasses clinked around the table.

A broad smile beamed in Sarah's face as the wine went down
smoothly, and the band began to play some melodies in the
background. She was having the time of her life.

The food was served, and more wine went around. But
something very funny was happening. Every time Sarah picked
up the glass to drink, she raised it and went, "Cheers!" In her

ignorance, she thought that it was a requirement to say, "Cheers!" before a person could drink at the table. In a move to save the day, Mr. Fosu followed suit, and soon, everybody joined in the fun galore. They all had a good laugh that evening over the perpetual clinking of glasses around the table. However, a little knowledge in table etiquette would have averted that awful faux pas.

Of much more importance is the knowledge of God. He has revealed enough of Himself and His ways to the world that no one has any excuse not to know and worship Him (Rom. 1:17–20). To ignore God and His Word is a terrible sin, and sin is an offense to Him. It is every human being's disease (Rom. 3:23), and it leads to eternal death. In the Old Testament, this disease was taken care of by sacrifices and offerings instituted by God in the Levitical law. Once a year, the high priest went into the Holy of Holies with the blood of a lamb to offer a sacrifice "for himself and for the people's sins committed in ignorance" (Heb. 9:7). But this was inadequate and temporary (v. 9). It prefigured Christ, our Great High Priest, who entered the Most Holy Place once for all, with the sacrifice of His own blood. He obtained eternal redemption for all who believe (vv. 11–15).

The days of ignorance are therefore past. God has finally revealed Himself to us in His Son (Col. 1:15; Heb. 1:1–4). He calls all people, everywhere, to come to Him through the reconciling work of Jesus on the cross of Calvary (2 Cor. 5:18–21). Anyone who ignores this call condemns himself before God; but he who accepts this invitation will be saved (Rom. 10:13).

Have you turned over your life to Jesus? Is He your Lord and Savior? Do you know His Word enough to walk with Him in knowledge and in deep fellowship? Can you commend Him to others who are still living in their ignorance and blindness?

For Reflection

For since the creation of the world God's invisible
qualities—his eternal power and divine nature—
have been clearly seen, being understood from what
has been made, so that people are without excuse.
—Romans 1:20

Prayer

Lord, remove my ignorance and spiritual
blindness so that I may behold the beauty of
Your countenance and grace in the face of
Jesus, the Lamb upon the throne. Amen!

CHAPTER 14

Ministry

1

Excuses, Excuses, Excuses!

Moses said to the LORD, "Pardon your servant,
Lord. I have never been eloquent, neither in
the past nor since you have spoken to your
servant. I am slow of speech and tongue."
—Exodus 4:10

I DON'T KNOW HOW many of us have sensed the call of God to ministry, and for how long, but are still denying, delaying, or outright refusing to yield to that call. There is always some excuse or reason why we think we cannot go when God sends us, so we struggle with it. But is it worth it? That's why I want us to consider from the examples of Moses, Jeremiah, and—you guessed it—Jonah. Like each of us, those men also had their reasonable excuses for their reluctance or perceived inability to go when God called them.

First, consider Moses. He feared his own past. He had moved ahead of God and caused a big mess in Egypt. As a result, he had taken refuge in Midian. When God called him from the burning bush, Moses' confidence was completely gone. The once aggressive and confident young man had been reduced to a doubtful eighty-year-old man by the harshness of his forty-year wilderness experience as a shepherd. He had lost any hope of ever returning to Egypt, let alone, to confront Pharaoh. However, that was exactly where God wanted him.

Unknown to Moses, God had used the wilderness to bring him to the point where he would completely rely on His leading. So when God called him out of the burning bush, Moses resisted. He had five strong excuses against his call. He questioned his worth (Ex. 3:11) and the value of his message (13). He doubted if anybody would listen to him (4:1), flatly stated his lack of eloquence (11), and finally asked God to send someone else (13). Those were all legitimate excuses for Moses, but were they defeating concerns for God? Absolutely not! God had everything Moses needed for the job, especially his meekness.

Then there is the prophet Jeremiah and his call. He also protested that he lacked eloquence and that he was too young for the job (Jer. 1:6). However, God was not challenged by any of that. He had already prepared Jeremiah, even before he was formed in his mother's womb (5).

How about Jonah? His refusal to go where God sent him was born out of prejudice, anger, and bitterness. Jonah could not bring himself to accept that God's mercy and grace could be extended to a "wicked and sinful" people like the Assyrians, considering all their atrocities against Israel. So he went toward Tarshish instead of Nineveh (Jonah 1). But as the psalmist says, "Where can I go from your Spirit? Where can I flee from your presence?" (Ps.139:7). Jonah eventually learned that "the far side of the sea" (9) was not enough to keep him from God and His purpose for his life.

That reminds me of my own experience. For about ten years, I tried to run away from God. I told myself that my friends may think that I had gone into ministry for economic reasons, should I say yes to God. Unfortunately, much as I tried to prop my fledging business up, nothing worked, until God confronted me one faithful morning after my devotion. He asked, "The opinion of your friends and that of mine—which is weightier to you?" I cried like a baby that morning. Finally, I yielded to my Savior's call in 1997.

My point is this: if God is calling you to ministry, the earlier you yield to Him, the better it will be for you. For there is absolutely nothing you can do about it. You can struggle to get away from it, but you will not succeed. The naked truth is that you will know no peace until you yield to Him. Yes, you may be making all the money, but you know how miserable you are, in spite of all that. You sincerely wish you could buy the peace you so earnestly desire, but it has eluded you.

The comfort and encouragement I can leave you is this: there is absolutely no excuse that God doesn't have an answer for, and there is no need in your life that He cannot meet. He is the all-sufficient God who is able to equip, protect, and cause His agenda to be fruitful when He calls. Just say with Isaiah, "Here am I. Send me!" (Isa. 6:8b).

He has already prepared you, so do not be afraid.

For Reflection

But they all alike began to make excuses.
—Luke 14:18

Prayer

Precious heavenly Father, I lay my fears and every
other excuse I have on Your altar. Help me to always
respond positively to Your call upon my life, and I
ask for courage and strength to fearlessly confront
every challenge for Your glory, in Jesus' name, amen!

CHAPTER 15

Spiritual Leadership

1

Do You Know Who You Are?

Jesus knew that the Father had put all things
under His power, and that He had come from
God and was returning to God; and so He got
up from the meal, took off His outer clothing,
and wrapped a towel around His waist, After
that He poured water into a basin and began
to wash His disciple's feet, drying them with
the towel that was wrapped around Him.
—John 13:3–5

IT TAKES A real man, who knows who he is, to be a servant to
his family and others, instead of being "lord and king" over
them. In the same manner, it takes a real woman, who knows
who she is, to remain in her godly position as servant in her
home, instead of being a "she who must be obeyed." This is the
lesson Jesus taught His disciples when He washed their feet before
dinner in John.13:1–17. It is the most practical and instructive of
all His teachings—the quintessential example and demonstration
of humility and selfless service.

Unfortunately, this kind of leadership is frowned upon in this world. People do not seek leadership to serve anymore. They lead to be worshipped. When people get the piece of paper that proclaims them as university graduates, they take it as deliverance from service and promotion to positions to be worshipped and adored. The village boy, who walked barefoot to school with some patchwork of khaki shorts and shirt, begins to think that he is too big to lift a finger at anything. The rural girl who carried a flat pan on her head to sell cassava in the mornings before going to school sees herself as "madam" with cuticles too precious to touch anything. Therefore, our homes and offices are overflowing with "lords" and "madams," so nothing gets done. Sad to say, Christians have become some of the most obnoxious offenders in this matter. Check out our pastors and you will see some of the most despicable acts of pride you can ever imagine. They have become too "anointed" to even carry their own Bibles. They have the so-called "Armor Bearers" carry them. God, help us!

Jesus saw the same tendencies in His disciples, so He taught them a lesson they could never forget. He washed their feet (John 13:1–17), a job reserved for servants in that Middle Eastern culture. If Jesus did it, we too can do it. But how did He do it, and how can we do the same?

First, it takes selflessness and humility to serve others rather than being served. Even though He is God, Jesus emptied Himself of all His heavenly prerogatives, took on the very nature of a servant, and humbled Himself when He stepped into our world to save us (Phil. 2:5–8). He saw His mission as one of service rather than being served (Mark 10:45). That's why, as His disciples, we are encouraged to have the same attitude (Phil. 2:5).

Second, it takes a person who knows who he is to be humbled enough to serve others rather than always sitting down to be served. Jesus knew who He was, where He had come from, and where He was going (John 13:3–5), so He was able to wash His disciples' feet. Serving others could not define who He was. Rather, it was a demonstration of the full extent of His love to them (v. 1). How about us? How do we show our love to others?

The world needs servant leaders like Jesus, not kings and queens, and Christians must lead the way. Jesus left us an example to follow (15), so when we fail to do the same, we demonstrate that we consider ourselves greater than Him (16).

May we not offend Him that way but be like Him who gave up everything to serve and to save us!

For Reflection

For even the Son of Man did not come
to be served, but to serve, and to give
his life as a ransom for many.
—Mark 10:45

You, my brothers and sisters, were called to be
free. But do not use your freedom to indulge the
flesh; rather, serve one another humbly in love.
—Galatians 5:13

Prayer

Lord, You are my Lord and God, yet You bent down
on Your knees to wash my feet. I am ashamed of
how proud I have become because of Your mercy

and grace that have lifted me to where I am. Spirit of God, strip me of all pride as You did John, the son of thunder who became the apostle of love when You took residence in his heart. May I be a servant willing to serve humbly in love! As I decrease to give way for You to increase in my life, may all glory and honor be Yours forever, in His matchless name, Christ Jesus, my Lord. Amen!

CHAPTER 16

Easter

1

Joy at Sunrise

Jesus said to her, "Mary." She turned toward
him and cried out in Aramaic, "Rabboni!"
—John 20:16

SOMEBODY ASKED ME, "Mary, why are you up so early? Why
are you so joyful this morning?" (John 20:1). How could I
sleep when the body of my Master lay in the tomb without proper
care? Don't you remember the events of two days ago—how
they crucified my Master who had done nothing wrong? My
own leaders did injustice to Him in their court and pressed for
His death in the court of the Gentile Governor Pilate (19:15). I
couldn't believe what I saw: the very people he fed and healed
shouted in unison for His blood. "But what has he done?" I
shouted, but their voices drowned out my query. They took my
Jesus away and whipped Him until he bled all over His limp body.

My heart sank when He came out, soaked in blood. Yet they
forced him to carry His cross and paraded Him through the
streets to Golgotha. They spat on Him like a dead dog and hurled
insults at Him all the way to the place of His death. Each time

He fell under the weight of the cross, they laughed and scorned. I cried, "Can somebody help Him, please? He is my Lord and Master." How glad I was when Simon from Cyrene came to His aid. May God bless him!

At Golgotha, they nailed Him to the cross (16–18). In anguish of soul, I shouted each time they drove those nails through His hands and feet, "Stop it! Please! Stop it, for He has done nothing wrong!" But no one listened to me.

He hung on the cross between two criminals. "Why are you doing this to Him? He is not a criminal," I shouted in dismay. But oh, the grace of my Master! Even in that condition, He forgave His tormentors. Stretched to the limits and dehydrated, He declared victory and died (28–30).

I wept uncontrollably. I wondered how I could get His body for proper burial. But, thank God, who takes care of all the details of His plans, Joseph of Arimathea, and Nichodemus buried Him in Joseph's unused tomb without proper embalmment because the Sabbath was upon us (38–42). That's why I got up at sunrise—to go and embalm the body of my Master. But I had the shock of my life.

The cave was empty when I got there (20:2). "Where have they taken my Lord?" I asked. "Can't they leave Him alone, even after they have killed Him?"

I approached a man I thought was the gardener and asked where he had carried the body of my Master. And, Jehovah be praised, the voice I cherish so much, the voice I thought I would never hear again, called my name: "Mary." It was so gentle and mild. I could not mistake His voice for anybody else. I turned and cried, "Rabboni!" I held on to Him and would not let Him go (10–17). Tears of joy ran swiftly down my cheeks. "No one is going to take you away from me again, Lord," I said.

Calmly, He told me not to be selfish but to go and share the good news that He was alive. Death could not hold him captive. The grave could not restrain Him in death. Jesus had risen!

So ask me again why I am up so early this morning, and I will answer a thousand times with joy, "Because my Savior lives!" Jesus is alive, Hallelujah!

Rejoice with me then, oh you people of God. Shout the good news from rooftops and mountaintops. Shout it from the valleys and plains. Declare the good news to all nations that my Savior lives, and because He lives, I can face tomorrow. Halleluiah, Jesus has risen!

Happy Easter!

For Reflection

For the Lord himself will come down from
heaven, with a loud command, with the voice
of the archangel and with the trumpet call of
God, and the dead in Christ will rise first.
—1 Thessalonians 4:16

Prayer
I rejoice that death could not hold You captive
and that, even in the grave, Jesus, You are
Lord! Help me, Lord, so that I may not be
selfish to keep this good news to myself
but to tell it everywhere I go. Amen!

CHAPTER 17

Suffering

1

Dealing with Adversity

But Naomi said, "Return home, my daughters. Why
would you come with me? Am I going to have any
more sons, who could become your husbands?"
—Ruth 1:11

WHEN THE NAME Job is mentioned, what comes to mind immediately is suffering. The old saint has become synonymous with suffering of the highest order, and by that, he has become the perfect example for the encouragement and comfort of Christians going through tough times. However, there is another Bible character I find very interesting to consider when faced with adversity.

Naomi is her name. She is a character in a small book called Ruth. Though Naomi did not suffer bodily afflictions as Job did, losing the three men in her life in a foreign country was no small ordeal.

Naomi had traveled with her husband and two sons to Moab to escape a severe famine in Bethlehem of Judah. After a little while, her husband, Elimelech, died. Her two sons, Mahlon and Kilion, took Moabite wives, hoping to fill their home with grandchildren for Naomi, so that she might have joy in them. But ten years later, they had no children. They too died and left Naomi bereaved of all the three men in her life. In that culture, it was a terrible situation to be in. Women depended on men for their sustenance. It is difficult to imagine her predicament today when women can make good living on well-paid jobs outside the home. So Naomi was lost completely in a foreign land.

She lived with her two daughters-in-law until news came to her that God had visited His people and provided food for them in Bethlehem. She decided to go back, and her two daughters-in-law decided to go with her. On the way, Naomi took time to consider, with the two women, their possible future lives in Israel (vv. 8–13). The noble woman that she was, Naomi wanted Orpah and Ruth to make educated decisions about their futures in a new country. They were young and able to attract new husbands and have children. Why tie their futures to an old widow who had very little hope for tomorrow? Orpah listened and went back home (v. 14). Ruth, however, determined to risk her life with Naomi, her people and her God, and anywhere she decided to live (vv. 16–18). Back in Judah, Ruth fell into favor with Boaz, a relative of Elimelech and a kinsman redeemer, and later got married to him. Their son, Obed, became the great grandfather of King David and ancestor of Christ Jesus. But how did Naomi deal with the adversity of widowhood and the loss of two sons in a foreign land? Two lessons stand out for our example and encouragement.

First, Naomi was a selfless woman who confronted her situation head-on without equivocation. She did not wallow in self-pity; nor did she play the blame game. Even though she described her situation as bitter (1:13), she was not bitter. Her life was so practical and real that it challenged her two daughters-in-law. They saw her kind heart and loving disposition. She became an excellent representative of her people in Moab, and that convinced Ruth to change citizenship (16a).

Second, in the midst of her ordeal, Naomi became a good ambassador of her God in Moab. Her faith and devotion to God shined through her life so much that Ruth embraced Him (16b). Everything Ruth knew about Israel's God came through the life of Naomi as she dealt with her loss, grief, and uncertain future.

The question for you then is this: when you go through adversity, how do you deal with it? Do difficult experiences and painful circumstances make you bitter, angry, self-pitying, blameful of others, and uncaring? In your moments of adversity, do people see Christ in you shinning brightest in raw, practical, Christian living? Do they see you display absolute trust in God?

That's the winning way for the children of God, and it is a challenge for all of us. It worked for Naomi and Job, and it will work for you as well. So can you trust Him in your current situation and allow His grace to carry you through to the brighter side and in His own time?

For Reflection

At this, Job got up and tore his robe
and shaved his head. Then he fell to
the ground in worship and said:
"Naked I came from my mother's womb,
and naked I will depart.
The LORD gave and the LORD has taken away;
may the name of the LORD be praised."
In all this, Job did not sin by charging
God with wrongdoing.
—Job 1:20–22

Three times, I pleaded with the Lord to take it away from me. But he said to me, "My grace is sufficient for you, for my power is made perfect in weakness." Therefore, I will boast all the more gladly about my weaknesses, so that Christ's power may rest on me.
—2 Corinthians 12:8–9

Prayer

Heavenly Father, I confess my weaknesses, pain, and anguish to You know. I need Your grace to keep me humbled and without bitterness that may cause trouble and defile many. Thank You for the example of Ruth, Job, and Paul, and help me to be like them in times of adversity, in the matchless name of my Savior and Lord, Jesus Christ, who suffered for my sake and can sympathize with my weaknesses and pain. To Him be glory now and forever, amen!

CHAPTER 18

Trust

1

Desperate Moves

"Look, I am about to die," Esau said.
"What good is the birthright to me?"
—Genesis 25:32

WHAT CAUSES PEOPLE to make decisions that lead to disastrous outcomes when they come under pressure? What entices people to throw away everything they have worked for just to get out of a little problem? Why do people make decisions that stand starkly against their faith when things turn a little sour for them? It's mostly because they get desperate to get out of a situation they may consider dire or critical.

In such situations, desperation causes them to push the panic button, and pandemonium breaks loose around them. Consider these examples below:

- It is desperation for survival that causes a mother to send her young daughter into the arms of an older person for the sake of money.

- It is desperation for marriage that causes a woman to say yes to a man she may not love, because she thinks she is getting too old.
- It is desperation that causes a person to take a job he doesn't like, so it messes everybody up in the process.
- It is that which causes people to travel to places they never dreamed of living.
- It is desperation that causes a man to sell his most treasured possession in order to live through the day.
- It is desperation for success that causes a student to cheat on his exams.
- It's desperation for fame that causes a young woman to sleep around in order to get a record deal, a role in a movie or play, etc.
- It's desperation for acceptance and recognition that causes people to compromise their beliefs and to follow the crowd and be caught up in their sinful and destructive ways.
- It's desperation for success and riches that lead people to embrace anything without regard for their faith or the holiness of God.
- It's desperation for numerical growth that entices churches to adopt marketing concepts that are purely worldly and thereby neutralize their impact in their communities.
- It's desperation for reelection that causes politicians to lie on campaign trails.

These are all because when a person is desperate, he doesn't think straight. Anything sounds good and appealing to him, so he will buy into anything.

Many people have embraced the Devil and continue to dance with him because they were desperate to get out of a situation that felt intolerable. It's all part of the Devil's tricks. He wants you to feel that your situation is going to drown you. But the good news is that you will not drown in that storm because Jesus is in the boat with you (Luke 8:22–25). It will pass like everything else, and when it is over, you will be standing alive and well because you trusted God and remained steadfast in His promises.

Remember Esau, who sold his birthright for a portion of red stew because he thought he was going to die from hunger (Gen. 25:29–34)? Later, he cried for it, but it was too late (Gen. 27:30–38). The disciples of Jesus thought they were going to perish in the storm, so in their desperation to save their lives, they panicked and even accused Jesus for not caring (Luke 8:24). How could they have perished in the storm with the Creator of the sea and waves in the boat with them? Unfortunately, that's what the Devil wants us all to believe when we are in tight situations. But if we trust the almighty God in every situation, we will prevail for His glory.

And so, before you hit the panic button in your desperation, stop and think carefully. Dispassionately consider the situation as it is. Don't embellish it. Consider the options carefully and where each will lead you. Check to see the godliness of every action you're inclined to take. See how it will impact your spiritual life. An option may not be sinful, but it could be a hindrance to your walk with the Lord. Consider the hand that is offering you help. It could be that of the Devil. Be prepared to suffer for as long as God wants for you to—He will never abandon you in midstream. Above all, pray much. Let the Spirit of God lead you through it all. You will never regret the result.

For Reflection

Moses answered the people, "Do not be afraid.
Stand firm and you will see the deliverance the
LORD will bring you today. The Egyptians you
see today you will never see again. The LORD
will fight for you; you need only to be still."
—Exodus 14:13–14

Do not fear, for I have redeemed you;
I have summoned you by name; you are mine.
When you pass through the waters,
I will be with you;
and when you pass through the rivers,
they will not sweep over you.
When you walk through the fire,
you will not be burned;
the flames will not set you ablaze.
—Isaiah 43:1-2

Prayer

I confess my fears and anxieties to You, oh Lord!
In my desperate moments, let Your assurances of
deliverance, of protection, and of Your keeping bring
me peace and stability, so that I will not make any
desperate moves that may cause me more trouble or
lead me astray from Your presence. Thank You for
answered prayer, in the mighty name of Jesus, amen!

CHAPTER 19

Contentment

1

Caught on the High Speed of Life

Watch out! Be on your guard against
all kinds of greed; life does not consist
in an abundance of possessions.
—Luke 12:15

"ARE YOU BUILDING again this year, Conteh?" asked an old buddy from college.

"Yeah, Ben! I can't continue to live in that small house anymore. Too much stuff these days. Need a bigger space. Since I bought the family van, my woman's car has been parked outside and that's not good. Need a three-car garage in this one. God's blessing, and I need some comfort to show it."

"I remember those days when we prayed about your finances in our meetings," Ben remarked. "But even then, I thought you were doing fine."

"You do!" Conteh exclaimed. "Remember I told you about the little project in the village? I needed some wind in my sail to speed things up. Couldn't keep Mama waiting, you know. She deserves some comfort, after all her suffering for me."

"And how's that going? Finished yet?" asked Ben.

"I handed it over to her in grand style, two years ago. It was a big bash with the entire village in attendance. You should have been there. And you know what? I have started my own project there now. Can't live in the family house when we go home, you know. We need the privacy," Conteh propositioned with a big smile.

"That's remarkable, old boy! I think congratulations are in order. You sure are moving up real well," Ben responded, with a pinch of sarcasm.

"Hold on, bro. That's just the beginning. I have acquired one of the estate houses in the Sodom Valley. It's a beauty, and I think you must see it. And I just acquired a property in the Gomorrah River Estate Project too. Exquisite! What else can a village boy like me ask for? You see why I work so hard, Ben?"

"That's right!" Ben agreed, with some cynicism. "But how does your woman think about all these travels and long hours in the office? You don't seem to be around a lot these days. She must be feeling lonely," he asked with genuine concern.

"Come on now, old boy. Where do you think all the fine clothes and jewelry come from? She can't complain. After all, all these properties are for her. I think she is fine with it." Conteh dismissed the question with childish ignorance.

"Well, I don't know about that. I have seen some pretty bad cases where you are heading. Remember the sermon of last two weeks? If I were you, I would slow down a bit. But that's me, from the old school," Ben advised.

"Not to worry, bro. I have it all under control. As for the sermon, I think the pastor was a bit off on some issues. Where does he think the big offerings and tithes come from? Can you believe he followed that sermon with an appeal for the housing project? We travel to make the money so that we can bankroll the special projects. That should make him happy."

"I think you got it all wrong, brother," Ben retorted. God wants our families together and functional for His glory. Look at our children, Conteh. How often do we see them? What do we know about their daily lives? Do we consider who they talk to about their struggles and the emotional burdens they carry around? And then we turn around to blame them when things go wrong in their teenage years. We are sacrificing our children, marriages, and personal health for what do not count in the realm that lasts forever. That's the point."

Very defensive now, Conteh shot back. "I have a God-given responsibility to take care of my family and to provide for their needs. They too have the responsibility to appreciate what God has given them and be thankful."

Taking a quick glance at his Rolex, he tore himself away from Ben with a lame excuse and got lost in the evening mall crowd.

He was in top gear, cruising on the highway toward the realm of fortune and fame until that tragic day in the hotel. He was found naked on the bathroom floor, with his hypertension medication by his side. The funeral ceremony was grand all right, but nothing went with him to the grave. Indeed, he had left a sizeable estate, but at what cost?

For Reflection

But God said to him, 'You fool! This very night
your life will be demanded from you. Then who
will get what you have prepared for yourself?'
—Luke 12:20

But godliness with contentment is great
gain. For, we brought nothing into the
world, and we can take nothing out of it.
—1Timothy 6:6–7

Prayer

Lord, I surrender my naked desires to You.
Tame my ferocious appetite for riches and fame
that has blinded me from the things that are
important in life: my relationship with Christ, my
family, and Your kingdom and its righteousness.
Give me grace to be content with what I have,
with a holy fear and godly attitude. Amen!

2

Complaining 101

"Sir," the invalid replied, "I have no one
to help me into the pool when the water
is stirred. While I am trying to get in,
someone else goes down ahead of me."
—John 5:7

I MAGINE THIS: YOU have camped out for the past three days
in front of your local computer store to buy the latest Apple
gadget. It is a limited edition and you must have it. The queue
is long, the temperature is bitter cold, but you do not mind the
wait. The gadget's review has captivated your imagination, so
the frostbite and the cold weather for the past three days do not
matter to you at all. This is the moment you've been waiting for.
Your life is nearly complete!

The store opens and the queue begins to move slowly.
Very soon, you will have your new "baby" in your arms and
everything will be all right. Just then, a van pulls up and some
cartons are taken away. The storeowner explains that the stock
belongs to another store and had been mistakenly delivered to
his store. Then the shock of your life comes: they are sold out
and you were only one customer away from the counter. What
a disappointment!

As you turn to go home, almost in tears, a man walks to
you and asks a simple question about what you want to do.
You vent your frustration on him, complaining about the cruel
treatment you have received in the weather and the unfairness

of the process. The man listens to you for the next twenty minutes, and when you have finished, he gives you the gadget with upgraded software that is not even out yet. He is Tim Cook, the CEO of Apple, Inc., and you don't even know. He asked you a simple question, and he received a twenty-minute lecture on complaining 101.

That was the story of the man at the pool of Bethesda who had been an invalid for thirty-eight years (John 5:1–15). Yes, he had waited for all those years for his chance in the pool when it was agitated, supposedly, by an angel; been left behind every time in the past; and no one had helped him during those times. Yes, they were unfair and hurting, but that was why Jesus was there. He had come so that he would receive not a chance at healing but the reality of it. Jesus asked him a simple question (v. 6), and he received a lecture on neglect and abuse (v. 7). But the loving and gracious God that He is, Jesus disregarded his complaining and healed him (v. 8).

You see, we have become a people who major in complaining. We complain when it is raining and when the sun is shining. We complain when it is hot and when it is cold; when the food is salty and when there just isn't "enough." We have become like the Israelites in the wilderness. If only we would see the bright side of things a bit, maybe we could better praise God for His mighty deeds in our lives.

Complaining is a sign of ungratefulness, and an ungrateful heart is a joyless and thankless heart, which is unacceptable in worship. That's why Paul tells us, "Do everything without complaining" (Phil. 2:14). It is the only way to be joyful and to worship God with a thankful heart.

For Reflection

I will forget my complaint, I will
change my expression, and smile.
—Job 9:27

Prayer

Father, I want to trust You in everything and to
be patient until You come through for me. Help
me to complain less and be more thankful for
Your mercy and grace that overcomes. Amen!

CHAPTER 20

Marriage

1

Bone of My Bone

The man said, 'This is now bone of my bones
and flesh of my flesh; she shall be called
woman, for she was taken out of man."
—Genesis 2:23

H IS EYES OPENED wide; his jaw dropped. It was the very first time he had seen and become aware of himself, and it was simply overwhelming. He looked around, and there was more—the sight and sound of his environment. Wow! What beauty!

There, before and around him, were the different sizes of trees and shrubs, a variety of fruits, and a variety of flowers in their beautiful adornment, filling the air with their delightful aroma. As he gazed on those wonders, trying to find out who he was, where he had come from, and where he was, his ears opened to the beautiful melodies of the birds and insects around him. Amazing! He closed his eyes and drifted away as nature sang to the glory of its Creator.

When he came to himself, he noticed some other creatures, huge and small, some creeping, and others walking on fours. Their voices, different in tune and intensity, added to the symphony around the garden, and it blew the man's mind away. "What's all this? What's going on?" Then he lifted his eyes to the heavens and—oh my! The beautiful sky, with all its inhabitants, stared at him. The entire constellation looked back at him with such warmth that he couldn't take it anymore. He dropped on his knees and raised his hands in complete surrender. He cried out, "Will somebody tell me who I am and what is going on here?"

As he continued in his survey of the beautiful garden with all its riches, Adam saw that every animal came in pairs of male and female. They snuggled, played, hugged, shared, and talked with each other. However, Adam had none of his kind to relate to that way. The concern and loneliness showed in his face as his joy ebbed away day by day. The Lord saw the burning desire in his heart, so He said, "It is not good for the man to be alone. I will make a helper suitable for him" (Gen. 2:18) Therefore, the Lord graciously put Adam under anesthesia, removed a rib from his side, and crafted a suitable partner for him.

When Adam woke up from his deep sleep, he couldn't believe what he saw. The most beautiful and precious of all of God's creation stood by his side. He had seen them all—the majesty of God's creation around him—but they were no match against this person standing by his side. His heartbeat increased in intensity, his hormones went through the roof, and his mind became woozy. Completely mesmerized and captivated by the beauty of his companion, Adam exclaimed, "This is now bone of my bones and flesh of my flesh; she shall be called 'woman,' for she was taken out of man" (23). And "the man and his wife were both naked, and they felt no shame" (25) living intimately and enjoying themselves in uncontested innocence.

Too bad we lost this innocence that enabled the closeness and intimacy of the sacred covenant between a man and a woman called marriage. However, it is God's will that you recover the purpose and joy of your marriage, the way it was in Eden. It is only possible with Christ Jesus as Lord and the willingness to yield to Him in all circumstances. If you allow Him (Eph. 5:22–35; 1 Peter 3:1–7), He will lead you and your partner back to the garden experience for the glory of God the Father! Believe it, for it is possible in Christ. Just give it a try.

For Reflection

Adam and his wife were both naked,
and they felt no shame.
—Genesis 2:25

Prayer

Grant me, oh, Lord, the eyes to see the beauty
of Your creation in my wife, and the ears to
hear her sweet voice in simple melodies. May
I never fear to bare myself before her, and may
You increase our joy in Christ Jesus. Amen!

2

When the Matching Disappoints

*His name was Nabal and his wife's name
was Abigail. She was an intelligent and
beautiful woman, but her husband, a Calebite,
was surly and mean in his dealings.*
—1 Samuel 25:3

I F ANY COUPLE could divorce for reasons of irreconcilable differences, it was Nabal and Abigail. Talk about night and day! Even their very names suggested that. Nabal means "fool," and Abigail means, "My father rejoices." So who will rejoice over his daughter's birth and turn around to marry her to a man called "fool"? How could a delighted father turn his joy into sadness that way, for that's all he could expect from such a marriage?

But wait, for there is something interesting to consider. The Bible says that Nabal was very rich (1 Sam. 25:2). The man had thousands of sheep and goats. So could that have been the reason for that misplaced nuptial arrangement? How does a person choose a life partner, and what happens when things turn out other than imagined? I will suggest three things from the Scriptures to guide us.

First, "Don't be unequally yoked" (2 Cor. 6:14–16). It is so easy to turn blind eyes and deaf ears to this command of God when the hormones are racing through the love bubble, but how true it is. Many have wounded themselves that way and put themselves in compromising situations.

Second, look for a God-fearing partner, one who is completely yielded to the lordship of Christ and His leading, not just a

"Christian." It gives meaning to Paul's exhortation in Philippians 2:1–2, which says,

> Therefore if you have any encouragement from being united with Christ, if any comfort from his love, if any common sharing in the Spirit, if any tenderness and compassion, then make my joy complete by being like-minded, having the same love, being one in spirit and of one mind.

That's your guarantee through difficult times, knowing that both of you will allow Christ to rule and direct the issues.

Third, prepare yourself for your partner in the marriage and look for someone who has prepared himself or herself in the same way. One of the worst situations is to marry a person who is not prepared to be independent of parents, physically, emotionally, financially, and spiritually, and be united in the marriage (Gen. 2:24). When that happens, every issue gets run back into the parental home, and that weakens the relationship.

If one gets these three basics right, the rest will fall in place, even though there will surely be challenges and, sometimes, serious bumps along the way. Your guarantee is not that your marriage will be trouble-free with these three factors in place. It is in the assurance that both of you will yield to the Spirit of God in seeking solutions and talking through your problems.

Notice I didn't mention money and beauty. As good and desirable as they may be, they should never be reasons for marrying. See what Abigail's parents did to her by marrying her to Nabal? So what if things just don't turn out right as imagined?

How we react to any situation will determine how things will turn out for us. Abigail may have regretted and suffered under the roof of Nabal, but she managed the situation very well. She reacted wisely and lived according to Peter 3:1–7. Her beauty was not only physical; she radiated a sweet, quiet, and gentle spirit that is of worth to God (v. 4). That inner beauty is what the servants saw, and that's what motivated one of them to speak to her rather than Nabal at a critical time when the entire family was in danger from an emotionally wounded David (1 Sam. 25:14–17).

Nabal was a "scoundrel," as the servant described him (17), but Abigail did not leave him. Rather, she held on to the sanctity of the marriage in honor of God and covered her husband's back even when he messed up (18–35). You want to know how she did it? The secret is tucked in a Scripture I love so much.

> But Daniel resolved not to defile himself with the royal food and wine, and he asked the chief official for permission not to defile himself this way.
> Daniel 1:8

It is only when we resolve to honor God in every situation that we can walk through the fires and the lions den to victory. We can infer that resolve in what Abigail did with Nabal. She purposed in her heart to honor God in their marriage, even though it was difficult. You can observe that just as God honored Daniel for his resolve, so did He honor Abigail in His own way.

God always gives grace for such situations, if only we can trust Him. Ultimately, He takes care of the problem. In Abigail's case, God took Nabal away (38) and gave her to a man after His own heart: David (42). I am not suggesting God will do the same in your case. I am just saying He has a way out for you.

Just trust Him.

For Reflection

No temptation has overtaken you except what
is common to mankind. And God is faithful;
he will not let you be tempted beyond what you
can bear. But when you are tempted, he will also
provide a way out so that you can endure it.
—1 Corinthians 10:13

Prayer

Lord, please give me a sensitive spirit and obedient
heart that I will determine to honor You in my
marriage and to bear under it for Your great
praise when things don't turn out too well.
Thank You, in Jesus' mighty name. Amen!

CHAPTER 21

Family

1

Love That Begets Love

The reason my Father loves me is that I lay
down my life—only to take it up again.
—John 10:17

IN THE EARLY morning of Wednesday, March 17, 2012, two sisters were wheeled into the surgical theater of a hospital in Dallas, Texas. One was urgently in need of a kidney replacement. She had been on dialysis for a long time and life had become almost unbearable. Only her faith in Christ and her tenacity kept her alive. The other had two perfectly functioning kidneys and was in good health. She had seen and felt the suffering of her sister over the years, so her heart went out to her. Nevertheless, she was tough on her ailing sister, who sometimes seemed absolutely unreasonable in her decisions and behavior. However, it was all motivated by love, and that's how it is.

When we love somebody, we stay close, get to know the person, and try to understand why he does what he does. Sometimes, we may even become a pest in that person's life, but it is all because we hate to see the person fail. That's a characteristic of love, and it is godly.

So when the time came for someone to donate a kidney to save the life of the ailing sister, all of the family members were tested, and guess who tested perfectly as a donor? The tough sister! Without hesitation or second thought, she volunteered to "lay down her life" for her sister in order to relieve her of her pain and give her another chance at life for the glory of God. No scrutiny by health officials could find any hesitation in her mind, nor could they detect any coercion from family in her decision. Her heart was completely yielded to the single and noble cause of donating a life-saving organ—one of her own kidneys—to save the life of her sister.

You see, sometimes, we talk big, promise big, claim big, and even swear big, but when the time comes for action, we flounder. It reminds me of Peter's denial of Jesus after all his big talk at the supper table (Mark 14:29, 39). Maybe he had had too much food and wine. That can make you speak without thinking. For when the time came to stand with his Lord, Peter denied Him three times (14:66–72).

Carina did not fail Christine. Amid the anguished soul of a mother witnessing her two daughters being wheeled into surgery at the same time, the anxiety of a father in far-away Dakar, and their other equally stressed children, the two sisters went in, smiling at each other, and knowing in their hearts what was sending them under the surgeon's knife: love.

Oh, the goodness and kindness of the Most High that never fails! He who is love and understands love, because He is the definition of love, honored the demonstration of genuine love by Carina for Christine, so He glorified Himself. The surgery was extremely successful, and a short time after the transplant, the kidney of Carina that had found a new home in Christine, began to produce urine. Isn't God good? Why wouldn't Christine love Carina? More so, why wouldn't God love Carina for her selfless display of love for a sister in need?

That's what Jesus did for us on Calvary. He laid down His life for the salvation of us who so desperately needed blood transfusion (1 John 3:16). By that selfless act on the cross, Jesus endeared Himself to God the Father (John 10:17). He commands us to love one another, as Carina has done for Christine, so that the world may know that we are His disciples (John 13:34, 35) and thus endear ourselves to Him.

Can you give your all, even your life, to let a dying world know that Jesus laid down His life to save and give us new life in Himself? (John 3:16).

For Reflection

And Jonathan had David reaffirm his
oath out of love for him, because he
loved him as he loved himself.
—1 Samuel 20:17

Prayer

Let me love as You have loved me, oh Lord,
and have given me Your only begotten Son,
full of grace and truth. May His unfailing
love move my heart to embrace others with its
warmth, and may I love them as I love myself.

2

The Beauty and Heart of a Mother

A wife of noble character who can find?
She is worth far more than rubies.
—Proverbs 31:10

I passed her on Ninku Street in Ogyakrom the other day, and something about her struck me. She was elegantly dressed, with exquisite jewelry gracing her long curvy neck and slender arms. The perfume she wore was mild but had a captivating, sweet aroma. I couldn't resist a second look at this gorgeously dressed lady. I whispered to myself, "God really makes exquisite sculpture."

"Watch where you are going, young man," said the man I almost bumped into as I stole a third look at the most beautiful creation of God I had ever seen.

"Excusez-moi, mon ami" was all I could say.

The man responded, "You French people are crazy when it comes to women. This is Ogyakrom, my friend. Watching a lady that way is offensive and could get you into serious trouble."

I sheepishly thanked him and trod away with a coy smile on my face.

Three days later, I met her again in my neighborhood. She was not dressed as she was the other day. She wore neither jewelry nor perfume, yet there was something special about her. I had never known grace in a woman before that day, for I was one of those men who foolishly thought women were just hair and legs. But I was wrong. God was revealing something to me for the first time with this lady. "What is it about her that makes her so special," I asked, almost aloud.

As if she heard me, she smiled and politely greeted me. "Bonjour, Monsieur Kemba." My jaw locked as I attempted a response. How did she know my name and that I was French? Frozen in my steps, I lifted my eyes into her big, brown eyes that waited for a friendly, reciprocal response. I managed a cursory "Bonjour, madame."

"Are you the French teacher at Tano High School? My son is in your class and speaks very well of you. We just moved here, and to get acquainted with our neighbors, my family is planning a cookout next Saturday. If you don't mind, my husband and I would love to have you come and share with us."

"Yes, it will be my pleasure," I answered, disappointed to know she was married.

"Three o'clock then. Our address is twenty-four Pokuase Street." With another smile, she extended her hand and bid me, "Bon journee."

Am I dreaming? I mused.

At exactly three o'clock, I stood at the door of twenty-four Pokuase Street, ready to be invited by the woman who had enthralled me for the past three weeks. But before I could ring the bell, the door opened and a huge man stood before me with a big, husky smile. "Come in, Monsieur Kemba." He ushered me to the backyard and to a table with six other neighbors who were talking sports. Still in shock, I set out to discover what made this woman so special.

The first thing I observed was that she and her husband were madly in love. The chemistry between them was enough to dissolve the slightest thought of romance I had entertained toward her. Throughout the afternoon, they made their rounds, stopping at each table to get acquainted with their guests. When one of the guys got a little off track with their maid, she swiftly intervened with uncommon dexterity and calmed the storm. I left their home that day with no doubt in my mind regarding how gracious and wise a woman she is.

Over the weeks, I observed how she brought her boy to school and participated in all activities, volunteering sometimes as substitute chemistry teacher. In PTA meetings, I was even more flabbergasted by her insightful contributions and suggestions. Every teacher in the school liked her. So now I know what made her so special: her beauty does not "come from outward adornment, such as elaborate hairstyles and the wearing of gold jewelry or fine clothes. Rather, it [is] that of [a] gentle and quite spirit, which is of great worth in God's sight" (1 Peter 3:3–4).

That's the ideal woman; the beauty and heart of a mother.

Happy Mother's Day!

❖

For Reflection

And she became pregnant and gave birth
to a son. When she saw that he was a fine
child, she hid him for three months.
—Exodus 2:2

❖

Prayer

I thank You, Lord, for my mother and all that
she has done for me, raising me and caring
for me through sleepless nights and difficult
moments. May I never forget her love but be
ever grateful to her for Your glory. Amen!

3

They Call Him Daddy

Children are a heritage from the LORD, offspring
a reward from him … Blessed is the man whose
quiver is full of them. They will not be put to shame
when they contend with their opponents in court.
—Psalm 127:3–5

H IS HAIR IS gray, almost faded from the center of his head and moving very fast toward the forehead. They call this process balding. He still cannot believe it is happening to him when he considers the countless compliments he received for the beauty of his hair as a young man. As a matter of fact, his wife confesses it was the one thing about him that set him apart from the other boys who came around her. But now, it is almost gone and all gray. Some say it is evidence of wisdom; others attribute it to genetic inheritance. Yet others claim it is evidence of abuse to the body as a result of hard work. Whatever it is, one thing is clear. He is not the same young and energetic man who charmed the most beautiful woman of their neighborhood anymore. His time has expired, and he knows that very well.

Gone are the days when his voice sent people running for cover in the house, the days when the muscles were strong and he was recognized as a symbol of discipline. He worked very hard, so he was almost always away from the house when the children were young. He loved his family dearly, but he never found the right words or the right ways to express it. Where he came from, a man did not show affection openly. That was a woman's thing, and a man was to be a man and different. So he kept his emotions under strict control. He hardly smiled, because it was considered a sign of weakness in his circle. For him, people had to see discipline and seriousness written all over a man's face if he was to be considered the man of the house, so he maintained that posture very well. However, deep in his heart, he was a soft man who was proud of his children.

Unfortunately, they never knew that. Nor did they consider him a loving father. For them, not being around the house was a sign that he did not love them. Even though he gave them everything and paid the bills, it was not enough. His wallet had become his most treasured attribute around the house, but nobody cared how it was filled. His children never stopped to consider why his palms were so calloused. They never considered what working two jobs, and late most of the time, had done to his body. Nor did they know that it was all for their sake, an expression of his deep concern for their future, and a demonstration of his love for them. To them, he was mean and uncaring—an absentee father. Why did they have to be tongue-lashed every time they asked him for something? Why didn't he smile or come to any of their games and other activities at school or sit around with them in the evenings, chatting the day away? Why did he have to be different? But all these were issues of his past. Things are different now.

The sun, the moon, and the stars have grown dark for him now, and the clouds have returned after the rain. The keepers of the house are trembling, and the once strong man is now stooping. The grinders have ceased because they are few, and nothing tastes delicious anymore. The eyes have doubled themselves because they have grown dim, and the ears are not as sharp as they used to be. The muscles give strength no more, but the walking stick helps him hop along like a grasshopper. And desire can hardly be stirred (Eccl. 12:2–5).

So today, as he sat listening to his son thanking everybody on national television but him, after been voted the MVP of the

Championship League, tears filled his eyes and a lump got stuck in his throat. "Hi, Ma. I love you," his son said, his face beaming with pride. "Thanks for being there for me." The father's heart sank at those words, and he heard himself whispering to his son, who couldn't hear him, "Did you ever have a father?"

Forgotten **A**fter **T**rying too **H**ard to meet **E**very **R**esponsibility. That's our lot, dads! You lose them when you try too hard. But for some of you young ones, it's not too late to make it right. Your children need you more than all the money you could ever bring home. So spend time with them, be in their pain and struggles, and laugh with them when they are rejoicing. It is okay to let them hear you say, "I love you," and to hug them when they crave it or every moment you are together. Then, maybe you will hear your son shout on national TV one day, "I love you, Dad! Thanks for being there for me."

Happy Father's Day

For Reflection

Unless the Lord builds the house,
the builders labor in vain.
—Psalm 127:1

Prayer

You only are the good Father, so I pray, Lord,
that You will help me to know how to raise my
children in ways that build their confidence and
trust in You, and joy in my home. Amen!

4

My Special Friend and Son

The woman became pregnant and gave birth
to a son. She saw that he was a special baby
and kept him hidden for three months.
—Exodus 2:2; c.f. Hebrews 11:23

THE FIRST TIME I saw him was in my dream. He was barely
visible behind the steering wheel of a nineteenth-century
automobile. The car was rapidly moving toward the edge of a cliff
beneath which was a deep and hungry valley that was yawning
and ready to swallow its tiny victim. Seeing the danger he was in,
I ran to his side and, somehow, managed to get into the car just
in time to stop it and prevent it from tipping over the cliff.

The next time I saw him, I was driving in the streets of Dakar,
Senegal, and there he was: cold and shivering in the early hours of
the day with his signature red tomato can in hand, begging in the
streets. With his nose dripping and his head covered with scabies,
he was barefoot and dressed in a filthy, smelly, tattered shirt over
a skimpy pair of shorts. My heart sank, and I couldn't imagine
how any parent would condemn their child to such deplorable and
criminal conditions as that. Unfortunately, this is the reality of
the religious landscape in Senegal. They call him Talibe, meaning,
a disciple of a koranic teacher. He is my friend and adopted son
at heart. If you want to see him, hit the streets of Dakar and you
will find him busily working the streets to make the amount he is
required to bring back to his master at the end of the day. In the
night, you may find him shivering in the cold, fearful to return
to his "home" because he couldn't make his quota.

But do you know what I see in his eyes every day?

I see a child loved by God and blessed with the possibility of living a full life in Christ. Given the opportunity (as IBC has given him and nine others in night school, hopeful that they may one day enroll at University Cheik Anta Diop), I see in him and the other Talibes doctors, engineers, pilots, lawyers, judges, or any top professionals you can think of. Yet they have been condemned to live in such deplorable conditions. The only opportunity open to my friend, and all the others like him, is to become, with the best of chance, a driver's mate, learn a trade, or become a champion wrestler if an alternative way is not opened to him. What tragedy to be limited to these ways in life!

That's what makes the mother of Moses so special. At a time when Pharaoh had decreed that every Hebrew boy that was born must be thrown into the Nile (Exodus 1:22), she fearlessly kept her son at birth because she saw that he was "a special baby" (2:2). As a result, God allowed her to raise Moses in her home and to prepare him to become His instrument for the deliverance of Israel from bondage in Egypt. What a mother!

Unfortunately, not every Jewish mother at that time saw what Jochebed saw in the eyes of her son, Moses, so their baby boys found their graves in the River Nile as Pharaoh had directed.

Today, millions of children are being voluntarily "thrown into the Nile River" and left to slowly die as child soldiers, child laborers, sex pawns, and what have you. They are robbed of what God intended for them to be in life, and you can see their sorrow and hopelessness written in their faces all over the world. What a shame on human dignity!

However, in the eyes of God, every child is special. Your child is special. Look in your child's face as Jochebed did, and you will see a smile that will melt your heart, because he/she has found comfort, safety, and hope in your arms.

So parents, do everything possible to give your children opportunity to accomplish their purpose in life, no matter how difficult you may think it will be for you to raise them. And may the Lord Jesus Christ, who said, "Let the little children come to me, and do not hinder them, for the kingdom of heaven belongs to such as these" (Matt. 19:14), strengthen and equip you in every way to make that happen.

Dedicated to all children.

For Reflection

If anyone causes one of these little ones—those who believe in me—to stumble, it would be better for them to have a large millstone hung around their neck and to be drowned in the depths of the sea.
—Matthew 18:6

Prayer

Our dear heavenly Father, help the little ones of this wicked world to grow in Your shadow and to grow to know Your Son, Jesus Christ, as their Lord and Savior. May I seek the welfare of the children You bring into my life, and as I do, may I be like a child before You. I thank You, in Jesus' name.

CHAPTER 22

Community

1

In the Same Boat!

The body is a unit, though it is made up of many
parts; and though all its parts are many, they
form one body. So it is with Christ ... Now the
body is not made up of one part but of many.
—1 Corinthians 12:12–14

ONE DAY, ASEREWA, a beautiful tiny bird in the tropical
rain forest, sat in the branches of a large tree singing in
appreciation of a beautiful day. Tucked under the same tree was
Mr. Tortoise, trying to rest and catch some sleep after a good
meal. However, Aserewa's singing made so much noise that Mr.
Tortoise couldn't sleep, so he decided to negotiate with Aserewa.

> **Mr. Tortoise:** Aserewa, can you please be quiet and
> allow me to catch some sleep? I am so tired and need
> to rest. Besides, I have a long trip coming up this
> evening, and you know my pace; it's so slow that I
> have to set out early to get there on time.

> **Aserewa:** And why should that concern me? I am
> having a good time praising God for a beautiful day.

If it bothers you, why don't you find another place to go and get your rest?

Mr. Tortoise: The shade of this tree is so comfortable for me. Besides, I am too tired to move any farther.

Aserewa: Well, that's too bad! Why should I stop praising God for such a beautiful day?

Mr. Tortoise: I tell you what. I will spare you your life if you stop singing for just one hour.

Aserewa: And how do you plan to do that? Can you climb up here and kill me?

Mr. Tortoise: No! But by my wisdom, I want to spare your life.

Aserewa (mocking): Your wisdom! Now give me some wise counsel, if you have any, and I will let you have some sleep.

Mr. Tortoise: Consider this: There is a hunter in the area and your singing could attract him to you, and you know the firepower he packs. Just a little silence, and he will go away from this area, then you can resume your singing. Meanwhile, I can enjoy a moment of peace in my sleep.

Aserewa (now really laughing): Is that your wisdom? What makes you think that the hunter will waste his bullet on me, such a tiny bird as I am? Besides, I am so tiny that I am almost invisible through the leaves. Even the best sharpshooter cannot get me.

Mr. Tortoise: Please, listen to me, before it is too late for you.

Just as the voice of Mr. Tortoise tailed off, the hunter arrived. He stopped right where Aserewa was and, with a sling, he shot Aserewa and killed it. Unfortunately, Aserewa fell just where Mr. Tortoise was, so when the hunter went for Aserewa, he also carried Mr. Tortoise away in his bag. You can imagine the conversation that would have taken place in the hunter's bag if Aserewa was not dead.

You see, no one is an island by himself. So long as we share space with other people, our actions affect them as much as theirs affect us. Sometimes, we Christians forget this truth. We forget that we are a community of believers in Christ Jesus and that our lives affect each other in every way. We forget that we are different parts of one body and that we need each part as much as Aserewa and Mr. Tortoise needed each other (1 Cor. 12:12–27).

May we find faith to believe in the commonality of our interest and to love each other as Christ has loved us (John 13:34).

For Reflection

If one part suffers, every part suffers with it; if one part is honored, every part rejoices with it.
—1 Corinthians 12:26

Do nothing out of selfish ambition or vain conceit, but in humility, consider others better than yourselves. Each of you should look not only to your own interests, but also to the interests of others.
—Philippians 2:3–4

Prayer

Lord, help me to be as selfless as You are and to
be mindful of my obligation to love and care
for the interests of others around me, as I expect
them to be so mindful and caring of me. Amen!

CHAPTER 23

Thanksgiving

1

I Am Thankful

I will extol the LORD at all times; his
praise will always be on my lips.
—Psalm 34:1

FOR ALL YOU have done for me, Lord, I am thankful. Who am I that the King of Glory should be so kind to me? Your goodness to me is overwhelming, and I cannot finish swimming in it through eternity.

Once I was a spoiled brat in my mother's house, in an obscure town in nowhere. In my misguided life, through the uncertain and bumpy terrain of school life, it is amazing to know how your gracious hand protected me. Out of college and with the world before me, my greed and pride took me on a roller-coaster ride through the streets of New York City in a self-destructive mode. Yet I laughed away in my ignorance and saw the stars from the "mountaintop." How deceptive and foolish to view the world from that "height" and see myself as all right when actually I was wallowing in the trenches beneath the earth! But even there, your gracious hand kept me.

As I trekked the world, declining real opportunities and going after the mirage of quick success in the business world, deceiving and being deceived, your loving kindness never left me. You led me through my self-chosen ignorant, deceptive, and arrogant life, always calling me away from it, always wanting to embrace me, without my giving you the opportunity. What a patient God you are! What a merciful King!

You did not have to protect me from my treachery, and you did not have to take my insults and abuses of your holiness, but your big heart bore with me. When I pushed you back, you kept coming after me until you led me to the gathering of your redeemed where I bent my knees to you as my Savior and Lord. At that point, I was broken. The light of your countenance flooded my life and dispelled the darkness around me when your loving arms embraced me. A recalcitrant sinner had come home at last!

Then I said, "I will repay you,'" but you smiled and said, "My son, it is free (Eph. 2:8–9). You are where you are because Jesus has paid it all. Just walk closely with me, and be my faithful witness to the world." Oh, the sound of the overwhelming living waters of the Most High God that floods the heart of the redeemed of His grace!

How can I appreciate you enough, oh Most High? With the fruit of my lips, I will thank and praise you all the days of my life. I will sing of your wonderful deeds and your unfailing love. Thank you for a loving and wonderful family. Thank you for the many children you have given me all over the world through the proclamation ministry of your redeeming grace. Thank you for the joy of witnessing lives transformed in your congregation. Thank you for the wonderful fellowship we share and your love that flows among your children. Thank you for tomorrow and all eternity. Let my heart continue to find contentment in you so that I will always flow in thankfulness to you, who alone deserves it, and may all heaven and earth resound with a big and hearty amen!

For Reflection

So he got up and went to his father. But while he
was still a long way off, his father saw him and
was filled with compassion for him; he ran to his
son, threw his arms around him and kissed him.
—Luke 15:20

Prayer

Father, I thank You for Your love, mercy, and
grace. I pray in the name of Jesus that You
will continue to pursue all those I left behind
when You called me out of the world. May I
never stop to lift them before Your throne of
grace until Your light that brings life dawns
on them. In His matchless name, amen!

2

You Too Can Be Thankful

One of them, when he saw he was healed,
came back, praising God in a loud voice.
He threw himself at Jesus' feet and thanked
him—and he was a Samaritan.

—Luke 17:15

L AST WEEK, I wrote a psalm of praise and thanksgiving to the almighty King, the only sovereign ruler over all creation seen and unseen. It was, and still is, an expression of my heart to this wonderful and gracious God who has been so kind to me throughout my life. I believe that if I am able to do so, you too can thank Him because you have a testimony that surpasses mine. That is why it is your turn to express your heart to the King of Glory this week.

Thankfulness is a state or condition of gratitude experienced by a person in response to a favorable gesture or situation. Usually, this condition cannot be contained without a verbal expression and/or action. In this sense, everyone can be thankful except the dead, for we are all recipients of favors of one kind or another. Especially when it comes to God, no one has reason not to be thankful, because we owe everything to Him, even our very lives.

In effect, claiming that you have nothing to be thankful for is claiming that God is not at work in your life. But may I ask you to check whether you are breathing, talking, able to walk, lift a hand, eat, smile or even frown? For these abilities all come from Him who made all things and "in whom all things hold together": Jesus Christ (Col. 1:15–17).

You may have been hit very hard by the economic downturn in your country, but you are still alive, knowledgeable, and healthy. Your paycheck may not cover all your bills, but it is still something. Your boss may be the meanest person, but you still have a job. Your apartment may not be grand, but you are not living in the street. Your child may be in prison, but he/she is alive and has a chance to turn around. They may have planned to destroy you, but their plans were thwarted by His unseen hand. You may even be living in denial that God does exist, but He has not killed you and His grace still bids you to "come home." You may be sick and dying, but you have angels waiting to carry you into His presence (Luke 16:22). Know that all these, and much more, are God's grace to you, for which you have to be thankful.

In Luke 17:11–19, ten lepers were healed by Jesus but only one returned to thank Him. He was so overjoyed that he came back to express it to Jesus. Because of that, he got more than he bargained for. He received salvation (19). The other nine received only their physical healing, but he received spiritual healing as a bonus. The truth is a joyful heart is a thankful heart, and a thankful heart is a fertile soil for more of God's bountiful blessings.

So this month, rejoice and express your heart in thanksgiving to Jesus in response to His goodness and countless blessings to you, your family, church, community, and nation. He deserves it.

For Reflection

But godliness with contentment is great gain.
For we brought nothing into the world, and we
can take nothing out of it. But if we have food
and clothing, we will be content with that.
—1Timothy 6:6–8

Prayer

Finding blessings in adversity is hard to do,
but help me remember, God, that You owe
me nothing yet You *chose* to give me so much
through Your Son, and that should keep my heart
grateful. Give me a change in attitude; let me
purpose in my heart to stop looking for You in
only the "big" things and find You in the "little"
things I so often take for granted. Amen!

CHAPTER 24

Encouragement

1

Needing to Be Believed?

> In a loud voice she exclaimed: "Blessed are
> you among women, and blessed is the child
> you will bear! But why am I so favored, that
> the mother of my Lord should come to me? As
> soon as the sound of your greeting reached my
> ears, the baby in my womb leaped for joy."
> —Luke 1:42–44

I T WAS A case of two women of extreme age difference, each needing affirmation. Elizabeth and Mary were both carrying babies under extraordinary circumstances and did not know who to tell! Who would believe that an old woman, well past childbearing age—with one foot standing in the grave—could have the other firmly planted in the delivery ward? Ridiculous! "Look at that old lady," they may have gossiped. "She wants us to believe she is pregnant. How people can deceive themselves!" "Will somebody tell her to get rid of that fibroid?" That's what Elizabeth had become—a public ridicule! So for the first five months of her pregnancy, she remained in seclusion (Luke 1:24).

What she needed most then was someone who could believe her, someone to throw her arms around her and whisper in an assuring tone, "I believe you."

There comes a time when all we need is someone to believe in us—someone to affirm us. You may be going through such a painful time right now. You have been misquoted and misinterpreted. You have been neglected and shunned as ridiculous. You have become a laughingstock among your friends and family. You are losing it and thinking of the unthinkable. If only you are standing on the side of truth, don't give up. The day is coming when you will laugh again. Divine help is on the way, and you will be encouraged. That day came for Elizabeth one gloomy day.

Mary, her relative from the town of Nazareth, came to visit. It was no ordinary visit. She shared the same burden Elizabeth carried in her seclusion: public ridicule. The top buzz around town was "Today's young girls—they can't keep themselves pure. How can she be pregnant when she is not married?" "Could that be Joseph's doing, that sneaky old man?" someone asked. "No, it can't be him. I can bet you a hundred shekels that it's one of those young men. Those little rascals," said another. "She never liked that betrothal anyway." With such talk, they may have chewed on her all day long. Who would believe her story? How could a virgin be with child?

Are people saying such things about you? Be sure that you are not alone. Someone else may be going through the same ordeal somewhere—or worse than you. More than that, your Jehovah is in it with you and will bring you in touch with a comforter soon. That's what Mary's visit to Elizabeth was all about—for the two to affirm and encourage each other.

You see, when you stand on the side of truth, heaven affirms you in every situation. Let everybody condemn you; God has someone who shares your story, one who has been through your crucible and knows how you feel.

That's what Jesus has become for us now, our Great High Priest who has suffered through it all and can feel our pain (Heb. 4:15). Your help is divinely ordained, and you will be affirmed soon. For as soon as Mary stepped into the presence of Elizabeth, the Holy Spirit filled Elizabeth.

In a loud voice, she exclaimed, "Blessed are you among women, and blessed is the child you will bear! But why am I so favored, that the mother of my Lord should come to me? As soon as the sound of your greeting reached my ears, the baby in my womb leaped for joy. Blessed is she who has believed that the Lord would fulfill his promises to her!" (Luke 1:42–45).

And Mary said:
"My soul glorifies the Lord
and my spirit rejoices in God my Savior,
for he has been mindful
of the humble state of his servant.
From now on all generations will call me blessed,
for the Mighty One has done great things for me—
holy is his name.
His mercy extends to those who fear him,
from generation to generation.
He has performed mighty deeds with his arm;
he has scattered those who are proud
in their inmost thoughts.
He has brought down rulers from their thrones
but has lifted up the humble.
He has filled the hungry with good things
but has sent the rich away empty.
He has helped his servant Israel,
remembering to be merciful
to Abraham and his descendants forever,
just as he promised our ancestors."

> Mary stayed with Elizabeth for about three
> months and then returned home.

Do you see the mutual encouragement two people who have been through similar situations can bring to each other? Do you see how each understood the other and how inspired they became in their speeches?

Maybe you are like Elizabeth, needing someone to believe you. Can you trust the Lord to bring you a Mary today? And while you wait, can you say a kind word to somebody who may be praying for an encourager to come by his/her side? A simple "I believe you" may suffice. Perhaps, you are the Lord's appointed minister to relieve that person of his misery today. And as you do that, may you be affirmed too!

For Reflection

> David left Gath and escaped to the cave of Adullam.
> When his brothers and his father's household
> heard about it, they went down to him there.
> —1 Samuel 22:1

Prayer

> Father, I thank You for the example of Elizabeth
> and Mary. I thank you that they understood and
> encouraged each other when nobody understood
> them. May I be an encouragement to somebody
> in need today, and may You strengthen us
> both as we stand in Your love toward each
> other. Thank You, in Jesus' name, amen!

CHAPTER 25

Christmas

1

The King Is Born!

While they were there, the time came for the
baby to be born, and she gave birth to her
firstborn, a son. She wrapped him in cloths
and placed him in a manger, because there
was no guest room available for them.
–Luke 2:6–7

I T WAS 11:30 p.m., and the young lady, tired from a long
journey and frustrated by a fruitless search for accommodation
with relatives and motels, finally settled for a place in a sheep
pen, where she felt the first pain of childbirth. A much worried
husband, very conscious of the baby his wife was carrying, asked
for a midwife. But before she could be brought in, the child had
come, a very easy and effortless delivery for a virgin who had
anxiously waited to see the face of the baby she had carried for
nine months, whose Father is from above.

As He burst forth from the womb of the young woman He
was to call mother, He took his first breath of the air He had
so carefully mixed for the sustenance of life on earth. What an

experience! The Creator of the entire universe had stepped into the world as a tiny infant like every human being He had created, and like every child ever born and born after Him, He cried for the first time to signal His arrival among men.

The air reeked of animal feces, and the breeze was dry and cold. His smooth, silky skin screamed for the warmth of some comfortable woolen and cotton cloths from His mother, but there was none. The one who made all things had to make do with some swaddling clothes as He was laid in a manger to take His first sleep.

As His eyes opened for the first time, the face of a beautiful young lady stirred intently into His. His mind raced quickly back into eternity to recall the time He first saw and knew that face. He had chosen this virgin, young lady from eternity past, and some few years back, He had formed her in her mother's womb and brought her forth for this very purpose. He smiled at her as if to say, "Thank you for believing that what the angel Michael told you would be accomplished" (c.f. Luke 1:45). A refreshing and warm feeling embraced the young mother, and smiling back at her baby, she whispered, "Thank you for favoring me this way and making me a part of your salvation plan. I am eternally grateful" (c.f. 2:46–49).

Over the shoulders of the young mother stood a delighted and proud husband who welcomed the child to be called his son, yet he knew very well he had no part in bringing Him into the world. What a scene!

In two distant locations—one in Israel and the other in the Gentile world—the announcement rang out. Some shepherds in the fields nearby had an angelic visitation and the honor of being the first humans to hear about the birth of the Savior of the world. With anxious minds and hurried feet, they rushed to Bethlehem to greet their Messiah (Luke 2:8–20). Later, representatives of a people "excluded from citizenship in Israel and foreigners to the covenants and of the promise, without hope and without God in the world" (Eph. 2:12) were to journey from the east. They would be guided by a star so they could come and pay homage to the King eternal, the Creator, and soon to be their redeemer and Great High Priest (Matt. 2:1–12). Even at birth, Jesus had made the two one (Eph. 2:14) and brought them together in their belief in Him.

That is the power and wonder of the Christ child who is born today and whom we celebrate and worship. The Creator of the universe has stepped into our world today, bringing all the love, mercy, and grace of heaven to us.

So celebrate the wonder of His birth, and rejoice that your Redeemer and friend has finished what He came this day to do on your behalf. He is continuing His ministry of intercession in your life from His position of authority and majesty at the right side of God on high and will soon come to fulfill His promise to take you into His heaven to live with Him forever. And don't forget to share this good news to your neighbor who does not know this love child called Jesus.

For Reflection

For to us a child is born, to us a son is given and
the government will be on his shoulders. And he
will be called Wonderful Counselor, Mighty God,
Everlasting Father, Prince of Peace.
—Isaiah 9:6

Prayer

Great is Your faithfulness, oh Lord, for You have manifested what You promised through Your servants, the prophets, for our sake. I rejoice to be a beneficiary of Your grace through the Christ child. Let this joy never cease, but that it will break forth in constant praise to Your majesty every day of my life and beyond.

CHAPTER 26

Praise

1

Praising the Lord

Therefore I will praise you, LORD, among the
nations; I will sing the praises of your name.
—2 Samuel 22:50

OVER THE YEARS and throughout history, great poems have
been written when the hearts of men and women were filled
with awe, wonder, gratitude, admiration, and even fear. Some of
those poems have become timeless, and some have warmed the
hearts of many people in different situations.

One of the best places to find such timeless poems is the
Bible. As you flip through the pages of the Word of God, you
can find such poems in the form of songs and prayers offered
in thanksgiving and praise to the Most High God. Usually,
these prayers and songs have been spontaneously offered in
response to God's amazing revelation; a glimpse into His
nature, wonder, and majesty; His holiness; and His mighty
deeds. The amazing thing is that even heathens, like King
Nebuchadnezzar, who did not know our Jehovah, have burst
into some of the greatest exaltation of God in praise after they

had experienced the power and magnificence of God displayed before them (Dan. 3:26–29).

Moses raised a triumphant song to God after the crossing of the Red Sea (Ex. 15:1–17) and at the end of his life (Deut. 32:1–43). Deborah praised the Lord in a song after the defeat of Sisera and his army (Judg. 5:2–31). Hannah glorified God when she presented Samuel to God in Shiloh (1 Sam. 2:1–10). David praised the Lord many times in songs recorded in 2 Samuel, the books of Kings and Chronicles, and principally, in the book of Psalms. Solomon, Hezekiah, Isaiah, Jeremiah, Ezekiel, and all the Old Testament prophets have authored magnificent songs of praise to God. Mary, Zechariah, Simeon, Anna, Peter, John, Paul, and many New Testament saints have expressed their hearts in praise and worship to the Lord when they were confronted with the holiness and majesty of the Almighty. The hymns we sing in our churches are filled with songs of the heart to God in response to diverse situations the writers were confronted with, for the glory of God. For example, Daniel lifted a beautiful prayer in response to God's revelation of King Nebuchadnezzar's dream to him, saying,

> Praise be to the name of God for ever and ever; wisdom and power are his. He changes times and seasons; he sets up kings and deposes them. He gives wisdom to the wise and knowledge to the discerning. He reveals deep and hidden things; he knows what lies in darkness, and light dwells with him. I thank and praise you, oh God of my fathers: You have given me wisdom and power, you have made known to me what we asked of you, and you have made known to us the dream of the king. Daniel 2:20–23

So have you seen God's majesty before? Have you experienced His mighty hand at work in your life before? Have you ever been overwhelmed by His love? Have you been a beneficiary of His provision, protection, and deliverance? Are you living today? Do you know how gracious God has been to you for just being able to lift your hands and move your feet to do whatever you are able to do; to see your children and your grandchildren? What is your response to Him?

Have you tried writing a song of praise to God? Can you write one to Him now? Come on, give it a try. And read it aloud after you've written it. Do that as often as you can and see the power of praise working in your life.

For Further Reading and Reflection

I will extol the LORD at all times;
his praise will always be on my lips.
I will glory in the LORD;
let the afflicted hear and rejoice.
Glorify the LORD with me;
let us exalt his name together.
—Psalm 34:1–3

Prayer
Fill my heart with praise, oh, Lord divine; Let
the joyful and ceaseless flow of heaven's grace
and mercy incite a loud anthem that echoes
throughout eternity for the Father's glory. Amen!